scratching

the

surface

Unlearning with Translation: A Critical and Collective Practice

Virginie Bobin

Sternberg Press

Villa Arson

Acknowledgments

I would like to warmly thank Sophie Orlando for her invitation to write this book, and for her precise, caring, and encouraging editorial companionship. I am thrilled that these reflections will circulate and hopefully elicit conversations under the umbrella of Scratching the Surface. I also thank Céline Chazalviel and Alice Dusapin for their accompaniment, and Villa Arson for creating the conditions for this book to exist. And I thank Andrea Ancira for being such an inspiring interlocutor and friend over the years.

This book is adapted from two chapters of my PhD dissertation *Au risque des autres: Political Gestures and Affective Encounters with Translation*. The research took place between 2018 and 2023 within the framework of PhD in Practice at the Academy of Fine Arts in Vienna with the support of doc.funds. I would like to thank my supervisors Anette Baldauf and Renate Lorenz, my external appraiser Tiphaine Samoyault, and my PhD comrades—particularly Eliana Otta, Serena Lee, and Olia Sosnovskaya.

Some of the reflections presented in this book are deeply indebted to the conversations and collaborations stemming from Qalqalah قلقلة, and I cannot thank Victorine Grataloup, Vir Andres Hera, Salma Mochtari, Line Ajan, and Montasser Drissi enough here—as well as all contributors to Qalqalah قلقلة's editorial and curatorial projects, and the institutions that have hosted and supported us since 2018.

Many individuals and organizations deserve to be thanked as well, including, among others, Mounira Al Solh, Mercedes Azpilicueta, Alix Eynaudi, Julie Faitot, Allison Grimaldi Donahue, Anne Kerzerho, Anna Leon, Barbara Manzetti, Julie Pellegrin, Rosanna Puyol, Emilie Renard, Barbara Sirieix, and Myriam Suchet. I also thank all participants in the workshops and seminars mentioned in the following pages.

Lastly, many of the projects presented here were made possible thanks to the support of my partner, Bachir; and of our mothers, Marie and Chantal, who cared for our children and for us on many occasions during this research journey. The love, joy, and wonder provided by Nour and Farah have kept me going throughout the past seven years.

A Movement Toward, and With, Untranslatability

> When I began to translate, I thought that I was prac-
> ticing an activity in the margins of the literary and
> intellectual world. I did not imagine that it would
> turn out to be an intensive, sensitive training for
> writing and ideas. Each text that I am working on
> imprints itself somewhere inside me and transforms
> my ways of doing. [...] I understood that, from the
> edges, one could do much more than what I had
> imagined. I found an agency.*[1]

I began translating after I had to leave my job at an art
center, worn out from months of conflicts, abuse, and
work overload. I began translating because I needed to
make a living, and I got carried into an extraordinarily
transformative and generative process, with deep intellectual, political, and affective implications. Around the
same time, in 2018, I joined the PhD in Practice at the
Academy of Fine Arts in Vienna.[2] My research proposal
was to study and perform different ways of working with,
and being affected by, translation and language politics in
the French context, as it is shaped by colonial and postcolonial histories and relations. In a global context where
language and translation are often used as tools of control,

---

1   Noémie Grunenwald, *Sur les bouts de la langue. Traduire en
    féministe/s* (Fives: La Contre-allée, 2021), 123–25.
2   I applied to this program because of its transdisciplinary
    approach to artistic research and cultural studies, and
    the practice-based, collaborative, feminist, decolonial,
    and anti-racist pedagogies that it advocates; and because
    it offered financial support to PhD candidates.

capture, and discrimination,[3] I wished to engage with translation as a situated gesture of address, informed by different affective and political registers. I wanted to test translation's potential as a method of unlearning pregiven sociopolitical orders and hierarchies; and as a critical tool for navigating, and acting upon, the contexts in which we live, learn, work, create, assemble, organize, and resist.

Over the past years working with translation—i.e., translating texts, with more or less difficulty, but also doing other things, such as forming collectives, publishing, teaching, or performing—I was guided by philosopher Barbara Cassin's definition of *les intraduisibles* (the untranslatables): "non pas ce qu'on ne peut pas traduire, mais ce qu'on ne cesse pas de ne pas traduire" (not that which we cannot translate, but that which we never cease to translate).[4] This definition suggests that translation is an ongoing labor: always incomplete, contingent, and situated; a movement marked by instability, equivocality, and open-endedness, as well as a gesture of attention and engagement. Meanwhile, I was aware that there exist more negative interpretations of untranslatability: since the dominant, capitalist order associates translation with

3   Numerous authors have written about the violent implications of translation throughout history. From a feminist perspective, I recommend Lori Chamberlain's excellent article "Gender and the Metaphorics of Translation," *Signs* 13, no. 3 (Spring 1988): 454–72. For the French context, Pascale Casanova's *La langue mondiale. Traduction et domination* (Paris: Éditions du Seuil, 2015) and Tiphaine Samoyault's *Traduction et violence* (Paris: Éditions du Seuil, 2020) offer great reflections.

4   Barbara Cassin, *Éloge de la traduction. Compliquer l'universel* (Paris: Fayard, 2016), 54.

transparency and access, it often perceives untranslatability or opacity as a threat, as these defy the possibility of knowing and therefore subjugating the other.[5] In eighteenth- and nineteenth-century Europe, the emerging discipline of translation served the formation of rival nation-states and their colonial endeavors, through "looting," "stealing," "appropriating," or "annexing" languages and their speakers—and the language I was raised in, French, played a significant role in that.[6] Many of my PhD colleagues came from places formerly colonized by these European powers, whose languages were repressed or replaced. Our relationships to untranslatability thus bore divergent implications and legacies, manifesting at times tensely through a contentious common ground—English.

5   Sarat Maharaj has explained how the notion of untranslatability can be instrumentalized by dominant groups and state power to essentialize difference and justify the implementation of racist policies for exclusion and control, as in the context of South African Apartheid. Maharaj, "Perfidious Fidelity: The Untranslatability of the Other," in *Global Visions: Towards a New Internationalism in the Visual Arts*, ed. Jean Fisher (Berkeley, CA: Kala Press, 1994).

6   In *La langue mondiale*, Casanova retraces the progressive establishment of French as a "world language," until it was dethroned by English in the second half of the twentieth century. She shows how translation was actively used to serve both the enrichment of language and the accumulation of capital *via* language, in a political context fueled by the ideology of a "natural hierarchy" between languages and, by extension, cultures and nations.

Staying with this trouble,[7] two authors have helped me articulate untranslatability into a generative method and practice while making room for its ambivalence. In her essay "Translating Positionality," sociologist and cultural theorist Encarnación Gutiérrez Rodríguez proposes we regard translatability and untranslatability not as diametrically opposed terms, but as a relationship, a movement, or a process, through which "ambivalent social and cultural positions are negotiated."[8] Building on her encounters with Latinx migrant women working as domestic workers in Germany—where her own parents had immigrated to from Spain in the 1960s—Gutiérrez Rodríguez unravels essentialist assumptions on how commonalities and differences are played out through gender, race, class, and language. For her, "translation procures understanding at the same time that it points to the potentiality of un-translatability." She insists on the necessity of acknowledging the gaps and frictions that emerge out of a double, concomitant movement of translatability and untranslatability, in order to create the conditions for a fairer encounter. Likewise, for literature scholar Tiphaine Samoyault—whose book *Traduction et violence* was an important companion throughout the last years—untranslatability signals not a blockage but an imperative: that of constantly going back over the

7   Donna Haraway, *Staying with the Trouble: Making Kin in the Chthulucene* (Durham, NC: Duke University Press, 2016).

8   Encarnación Gutiérrez Rodríguez, "Translating Positionality: On Post-Colonial Conjunctures and Transversal Understanding," *Transversal*, June 2006, https://transversal.at /transversal/0606/gutierrez-rodriguez/en.

labor of translation, of tending to its ambivalence and risks, while preserving its inherent opacity.[9] In doing so, it becomes possible to debunk an understanding of translation as a call for transparency and as a tool for capture, thus creating the conditions for a more ethical practice of translation. The book that you are holding emerged out of a series of attempts to exercise this practice with others.

*

Translation not only put me in contact with incredible texts and authors. It also transformed how I learn, write, and work. It began to permeate many different moments of my life, even when I was doing something completely other than translation. While changing diapers or walking through the forest, a word that I had been looking for suddenly appeared at the surface of my distracted mind. Cooking with loved ones, we discussed the political implications of choosing one term over another, and the decisions that were made by other translators before us. Writing a funding application, a project proposal, a letter, or a petition, translation became a vehicle to think and act with the words of others. Self-organizing, teaching, or performing, translation offered a method for doing things with companions, students, and comrades. It allowed me to engage in the assemblage of communities through collective translation projects and pedagogical experiments. During a series of conversations that I initiated with interpreters working in the field of asylum

9   Samoyault, *Traduction et violence*.

rights in Europe, a self-taught interpreter and translator once told me: "Doing translations helped me find some very close friends."[10] I couldn't agree more.

Among the friendships woven through translation over the past years, I am deeply indebted to the collective that formed around Qalqalah قلقلة, an editorial and curatorial platform that I co-founded with curator Victorine Grataloup in 2018, in reaction to a political and intellectual context marked by reactionary, authoritarian, and discriminatory speeches and acts. Qalqalah قلقلة built itself through a series of workshops, events, and conversations, and was soon joined by curator Line Ajan, graphic designer Montasser Drissi, artist Vir Andres Hera, and curator and researcher Salma Mochtari. Each of us found in Qalqalah قلقلة a base from which to develop personal and collective lines of inquiry while learning from our respective experiences and positions, and from the tensions and disagreements that are part of collective work. As we wrote in our introduction in 2020, Qalqalah قلقلة

> relies on translation as a tool for the production and reception of situated knowledge, capable of making visible the relations of power and the possibilities of invention and affection that are at play between languages, temporalities and contexts that are marked by the colonial legacy, conflicts and contemporary revolts. [...] More than a publishing space, Qalqalah قلقلة is conceived as a place of attachments, where one can cultivate long-lasting

10 This work gave birth to another book: Virginie Bobin, *The Interpreter Dis/Appears* (Berlin: Scriptings, forthcoming).

friendships, generative connections and multiple affections.[11]

As far as I am concerned, Qalqalah قلقلة became a vital place for discussing, deepening, and experimenting with the affective and political stakes of translation. This happened through various means: invitations extended to thinkers and scholars; making exhibitions that allowed us to interact with artists and display various formal and theoretical approaches to translation and language politics; workshops and seminars that offered possibilities to test collective learning formats and share our questions with other students and researchers; editorial work that required close engagement with texts and ideas; as well as translation, of course, as we often translated the platform's content ourselves. It was also facilitated by formal and informal gatherings and discussions with the collective. In parallel, a growing community of friends, artists, and researchers formed around Qalqalah قلقلة as we strived to maintain lasting collaborations and conversations to defend ourselves against political violence, loss, and precarity—in a context marked by the Covid-19 pandemic, the international rise of the far right, and the genocide in Gaza and its global repercussions, among other dramatic events.

*

11   See https://qalqalah.org/en/about-qalqalah (last accessed March 12, 2025).

This book was written over the course of several years: first as my PhD in Practice dissertation, submitted in 2023 under the title *Au risque des autres: Political Gestures and Affective Encounters with Translation*.The first part of the title quotes Isabelle Stengers: in *Résister au désastre* (Resisting disaster) and several other essays, the philosopher insists on the necessity of "doing with others, or doing thanks to others, and at the risk of others."*[12] Following Stengers, we should let ourselves be affected and transformed in our implications with others, in order to think and act in ethical ways. I recognized in this call a possible model for a hospitable, vulnerable, and caring practice of translation. Furthermore, Stengers advocates for a practice-based relationship to "doing-knowing" where knowledge is shaped, transformed, and shared through ongoing gestures and encounters rather than on the basis of ideas. This is a method I have tried to embody throughout my research and I am hoping to extend with this book.

When Sophie Orlando invited me to contribute to the series Scratching the Surface, in the framework of a research project on critical pedagogies hosted by Villa Arson, I was still in the process of writing my dissertation. Imagining an audience for this text, especially tied to an art-school context and to a critical reflection on pedagogy, was a tremendous motivation: it allowed me to project future activations and reinterpretations onto the gestures that I was writing about in conversation with students, teachers, and peers. It also led me to focus on the critical

---

12   Isabelle Stengers, *Résister au désastre. Dialogue avec Marin Schaffner* (Marseille: Wildproject, 2019), 25.

notion of unlearning, which forms the backbone of one of the ensuing essays and which became a prism through which I selected and shortened the parts adapted for this book. I wrote it in the summer of 2023 and revisited it in February 2025, following a year-and-a-half-long stasis related to administrative and budgetary circumstances. Since 2023, many incredible thinkers, authors, and translators have advanced further reflections on translation, which has gained a certain visibility as a public, political concern.[13] It was not possible to belatedly include all these voices within this book, which is conceived as a temporary configuration of gestures to be criticized, reinterpreted, and updated—but I would still like to acknowledge their nurturing presence.

13 One important example is Maboula Soumahoro's translation of Saidiya Hartman's *Lose Your Mother: A Journey Along the Atlantic Slave Route* (New York: Farrar, Straus and Giroux, 2007), published as *À perte de mère – Sur les routes atlantiques de l'esclavage* (Paris: Brook, 2023). In her preface, Soumahoro proposes a situated, decolonial approach to translating blackness, grounded in a quest for already exisiting terms —"missing words, silenced words, which nevertheless exist"* (10). I am also thinking about the *Funambulist*'s commitment since 2023 to publishing French and Spanish versions of the magazine alongside the original English, and about its fifty-third issue "Thread of Translations" (2024), featuring thirty translations into "non-hegemonic" languages of a text by Indigenous Mixe writer Yásnaya Elena Aguilar Gil. As part of the team of translatresses for the French version, I am indebted to my ongoing conversations with Rosanna Puyol Boralevi, Caroline Honorien, Amina Belghiti, and Leopold Lambert about the political implications of translating terms and positionalities that stem from very different contexts and experiences.

This book wishes to act as a loving witness to the bonds, arguments, doubts, and relationships proliferating through translation. It was written while tending to a garden, learning how to care for the plants, the animals, and the river sharing the space with us, in the rural area I moved to several years ago—a situation that deeply reconfigured my engagement with artistic labor and its economy of presence and visibility, among many other things. It was written throughout the course of my second pregnancy, marked by mourning and depression, and while caring for two young children day after day, night after night—sleep-deprived, interrupted, stained, and radically loved. It was written in a state of wonder, caused by the emergence of, and intense curiosity for language in these two beings, and by the forging of a renewed feminist consciousness among mothers, parents, and allies in the face of a largely unfavorable labor ecosystem in the arts. It was written, at last, thanks to the salary that I received from the Academy of Fine Arts in Vienna during the four years of my PhD research, which provided me with the all too rare possibility of being financially able to fully commit to study.[14]

14   Fred Moten describes "study" as follows, in a conversation with Stefano Harney and Steven Shukaitis: "I think we are committed to the idea that study is what you do with other people. It's talking and walking around with other people, working, dancing, suffering, some irreducible convergence of all three, held under the name of speculative practice. The notion of a rehearsal—being in a kind of workshop, playing in a band, in a jam session, or old men sitting on a porch, or people working together in a factory—there are these various modes of activity. The point of calling it 'study' is to mark that the incessant and irreversible

Apart from this introduction, the book includes two essays and a correspondence with Andrea Ancira, which can be read as standalone texts or in succession. The first essay, "Word Battles and Counter-Glossaries," was born out of the anger and anxiety resulting from what philosopher Marie José Mondzain has called the "confiscation of words, images, and ideas"* by representatives of the reactionary, neoliberal order that pervaded our daily lives in France at the time of my research, from 2018 to 2023.[15] It was written as a possible antidote to the racist, heteropatriarchal, exclusionary logics that proliferate through biased language and vocabularies, as translation productively reveals by suspending our unquestioned adherence to words and discourses. It was written in English for an international readership (i.e., my PhD comrades and teachers) not necessarily familiar with the French context, out of the urge to critically map out the territory in which the different protagonists in this book work with translation.

The second essay, "Unlearning with Others," revisits various experiments with, and discussions about, translation and untranslatability. Here translation is introduced as a collective gesture of unlearning, inspired by critical thinkers of education and culture such as

intellectuality of these activities is already present. [...] To do these things is to be involved in a kind of common intellectual practice." Moten, in *The Undercommons: Fugitive Planning & Black Study* (Wivenhoe: Minor Compositions, 2013), 110.

15 Marie José Mondzain, *Confiscation des mots, des images et du temps. Pour une autre radicalité* (Paris: Les liens qui libèrent, 2017).

Gayatri Chakravorty Spivak, bell hooks, Fred Moten and
Stefano Harney, and Ariella Aïsha Azoulay. Alongside
their theoretical insights, this essay builds on practical
"translation problems" to turn translation into a subject
of investigation, a situated critical practice, and an artistic, theoretical, and political tool for doing things with
others. This approach to translation irrigates "Where We
Stand, Where We Slip," my correspondence with editor,
researcher, and translator Andrea Ancira, who has been a
dear friend and intellectual and political companion since
2016. Written between October 2024 and February 2025,
in the interstices of various personal and political struggles, our letters tend to the generative tensions in which
our working and living practices are embedded.

*

Finally, this book was written in between two languages:
French*es*, my native language, an imperial language that
was enforced in various parts of the world through col-
onization, the language I speak with my children; and
English*es*, another imperial language, in which I encountered most of the theories that have nurtured this
research,[16] and in which incredibly generative friendships
blossomed over the last years. It was also written in the
presence of several other languages, including Spanish*es*,

---

16   It is crucial to note that the scope of my research is narrowed
       by the two languages in which I was able to access theory:
       English and French. This effectively cut me off from other,
       notably non-Western approaches and epistemologies
       that have escaped translation into either of these languages.

through my collaboration with Mercedes Azpilicueta; and Arabic*s*, a language which I have tried to learn (and failed so far), a language that is often discriminated against in the French context, a language that bears, for my family, a history of loss and longing. These languages are written and spoken in plural, following researcher Myriam Suchet's invitation to read the "s" at the end of *français* as a mark of plurality. As she reminds us, "French [and other languages for that matter] does not exist."* For her, *"la langue"*—language, which she always refers to in quotation marks to signal the incongruity of the definite article in French—"only exists according to the spoken words that make and unmake it [...] woven with voices, accents and all sorts of inputs."*[17] Writing the book in Englishes, later translating—or rather rewriting—myself into Frenches, reflected the constant round trips I had to undertake between languages, regimes of knowledge, theoretical discourses, and affective relations: an ongoing process of untranslation.

June 2023
(revisited in February 2025)

17   Myriam Suchet, *Traduire du français aux français*, no. 1 (Rennes: Éditions du commun, 2021).

Word Battles and Counter-Glossaries: A View of the Territory in Which the Translatress Maneuvers[18]

18   The subtitle is a quote from translation theorist Sherry Simon, as she reflects on the situated practice of feminist translatresses who undertake forms of critical writing in dialogue with their translations: "In mapping out the cognitive and affective components of translation, they provide a view of the territory within which the translator maneuvers." Simon, *Gender in Translation: Cultural Identity and the Politics of Translation* (New York: Routledge, 1996), 35–36.

Have you ever felt anger or anxiety caused by the misappropriation, misinterpretation, or misuse of certain words that are becoming omnipresent in the public discourse? Have you ever shuddered with rage or fear when certain words that you consider guiding principles become targeted, or are used to target you, the individuals and organizations that you care for? There are the words that we cherish, care for, and cling on to, because they map the contours of desired realities and serve as anchoring points for our alliances and encounters: *care, feminist, intersectional, decolonial, ecology*, just to name a few. And there are the words that obscure these realities, separate, delegitimize, hurt, threaten, and exclude—*separatism, national identity*, and biased uses of *secularism*, for instance, not to mention the whole lexicon of racist, sexist, homophobic, transphobic, ableist, and other discriminatory speech acts. Have you ever felt the weight and power of these words overflowing media spaces, political debates, and legal texts? And the vulnerability or even danger of other ones, which may cause the defunding of your university program, the rejection of your job application, insults and threats. Have you ever felt compelled, or been asked to look for a more "nuanced" synonym? Have you ever mourned the disappearance, erasure, or censorship of certain words? Does it make you afraid? Does it make you sick? Does it make you want to organize and resist? How?

In her book *Living a Feminist Life*, Sara Ahmed explains how it is impossible to unsee sexism and racism once one has started to notice them.[19] For her, the ongoing labor of naming and calling attention to problems—which are so embedded in social structures that pointing to them is perceived as a threat to the dominant status—is political. I would argue that translation does a similar kind of work: reflecting on the transposition of certain terms into different contexts, one is forced to unpack their ideological, political, and affective implications, thus unearthing the social structures and discourses in which they are embedded at a given moment. In doing so, we are calling attention to problems—good or bad—that these words, and their uses, carry. Through the decentering lenses provided by other languages, contexts, and positions, we are unlearning the neutrality, stability, and innocuousness of words that are taken for granted. It's a first step.

I began to translate on a regular basis in 2018, one year after the election of President Macron, whose government accelerated the neoliberalization of politics and paved the way for the rise of the far right in France—in line with what has been happening on a global scale. French writer Sandra Lucbert—and numerous other authors[20]—analyzed the transformation of public, political, and legal speech during the 2010s in her chilling *Personne ne sort les fusils.* The book dissects the 2019 trial of seven France Télécom managers who orchestrated a series of abusive measures as part of a large-scale, undercover redundancy

19   Sara Ahmed, *Living a Feminist Life* (Durham, NC: Duke University Press, 2017).

20   See for example, Selim Derkaoui and Nicolas Framont, *La guerre des mots. Combattre le discours politico-médiatique de la bourgeoisie* (Lorient: Le Passager Clandestin, 2020).

scheme, which led to nineteen suicides.[21] Lucbert analyzes the dehumanization of society via the dissemination of "a liquid language that does not stick"*—a global managerial jargon that distorts reality and perpetuates violence under the guise of performance and progress. Lucbert ironically calls this language LCN (*Lingua Capitalismi Neoliberalis*), which she describes as "a *hegemonic language*. A set of utterances that transform a relationship of domination toward an entire social body."*[22]

LCN makes direct reference to Victor Klemperer's LTI (*Lingua Tertii Imperii*, or Language of the Third Reich), a new, totalitarian language, which the German Jewish scholar analyzed in his diaries between 1933 and 1945.[23] The point here is not to draw a comparison between the political situation in France in the first decades of the twenty-first century and the Nazi era;[24] it is to learn from Klemperer's linguistic study of how language can be twisted in order to disseminate a specific ideology, driven by the will to control a given social body according

21   Sandra Lucbert, *Personne ne sort les fusils* (Paris: Éditions du Seuil, 2020).

22   Sandra Lucbert, "La littérature contre l'ordre hégémonique : attaquer sa langue." interview by Noémie Cadeau, *Le Vent Se Lève*, October 20, 2020, https://lvsl.fr/la-litterature -contre-lordre-hegemonique-attaquer-sa-langue-entretien -avec-sandra-lucbert/.

23   It appeared in English as *Language of the Third Reich: LTI, Lingua Tertii Imperii; A Philologist's Notebook*, trans. Martin Brady (London: Continuum, 2005).

24   Lucbert justified the analogy in several interviews by the repeated evocations, in French media of all persuasions, of World War II and the Nuremberg trials to describe the France Télécom trial, which she found significative on both political and psychoanalytical levels.

to certain dividing lines. Indeed, for Klemperer, LTI did not contribute to the propagation and acceptance of Nazi ideology by producing new words; rather, it modified the values associated with certain words and intensified their use until they impregnated all parts of German society, including those who attempted to resist said ideology.

Klemperer dedicated a significant part of his study to the change of values applied to "fanatical," which became charged with virtuous connotations under Nazi domination. Today, the term is commonly associated with Islamic fundamentalism in international media and public discourse. It carries the fear of terrorism and another belligerent rhetoric—that of the war on terror. In France, this rhetoric took on a new scope in 2015, after a series of deadly attacks in Paris relocated that war to domestic soil, leading up to the legal promulgation of the state of emergency.[25] The same linguistic strategies that Klemperer had scrutinized were activated here. Certain words were repeatedly mobilized to sustain a state narrative based on a fictitious ideal of enlightened republican secularism under threat of "separatism." In an essay commissioned by Qalqalah قلقلة, in which she notably analyzed the 2021 "separatism law,"

---

25   The state of emergency law was promulgated for the first time in 1955, during the period leading up to the Algerian War of Independence. It is thus anchored in a colonial heritage that implicitly resurfaced through the subsequent reactivations of the law in 2005 (when protests erupted in the French suburbs after two racialized teenagers, Zyed Benna and Bouna Traoré, electrocuted themselves while fleeing police); and from 2015 to 2017 following the terror attacks in Paris. In November 2020, a new law declared a "sanitary state of emergency" in response to the Covid-19 pandemic.

sociologist Houda Asal explained that "the provisions proscribing 'separatism' do not target groups fomenting violent acts, but religious, cultural and political practices perceived as anti-republican."[26]

These observations, and the necessity to equip ourselves both politically and intellectually in the face of this "war of words," played a great part in motivating Victorine Grataloup and myself to revive Qalqalah قلقلة in 2018.[27] The name Qalqalah قلقلة comes from two short stories by Egyptian curator and researcher Sarah Rifky.[28] The eponymous heroine of these works of fiction, Qalqalah, is an artist and linguist who inhabits a near future transformed by the 2008 financial crisis and the popular revolts of the 2010s. Our intuition was that, by taking Qalqalah's questions about language and translation seriously, we would be able to better resist the debilitating, exclusionary effects of such narratives and reclaim confiscated words. As Rifky later wrote in an essay published in March 2020, just a few days before the public launch of our online platform amid the Covid-19 pandemic: "To think

26   Houda Asal, "From Islamophobia to Separatism: What the War of Words Reveals," (2022), trans. Mary Foster, Qalqalah قلقلة, https://qalqalah.org/en/essays/from-islamophobia-to-separatism.

27   An earlier version of Qalqalah, in which both Victorine and I were involved, had been initiated in Paris by Bétonsalon – Center for Art and Research and Kadist Art Foundation, and was active from 2015 to 2017.

28   Sarah Rifky, "Qalqalah: The Subject of Language" (2015), Qalqalah قلقلة, https://qalqalah.org/en/histories/qalqalah-the-subject-of-language; and Rifky, "Qalqalah: Thinking About History" (2016), Qalqalah قلقلة, https://qalqalah.org/en/histories/qalqalah-thinking-about-history.

about language at a time like this seems scholastic, but it really isn't. To call a thing by its name can help reframe the problem—and the imagination."[29] Let's take a small detour and follow Qalqalah's voice for a while, as it transits through a multitude of authors and languages ...

*

"Do you know what your name means?" The writer asks, her voice burnished and unplaceable. The writer defines her name with strange sounds. She will cache these sounds for years and later learn that they are meanings in different languages: names for bitter qualities, minor stars, a variety of spouted earthen vessel, and the evasive flicker of a cat that is not a metaphor.[30]

Every day, Qalqalah gets up to face the rest of her life, a life post-narrative. In her recollection of stories, she never takes language for granted. Today, as she wakes up, she tries to understand the paradigm of "monolingual activism" of a group of people she had met outside of convention seeking to invent a new polity with the help of linguists and financiers. She rightfully reasons that at the heart of any mono-lingual impulse is a questioning of the hegemony

29 Sarah Rifky, "reimagine: all the people," *Mada Masr*, March 27, 2020, https://www.madamasr.com/en/2020/03/27 /opinion/u/reimagine-all-the-people/.
30 Serena Lee, "Qalqalah: Tempo Rubato" (2020), Qalqalah قلقلة, https://qalqalah.org/en/histories/qalqalah-tempo-rubato.

of imperial language. She pauses to rethink her thought in a language outside of English. It is a repetitive thought. She pauses again to rethink her thoughts in a language external to French. The pauses continue until she has rethought her thoughts in the spectrum of languages known to her. The feeling associated with each thought was distinct from the other thoughts, even though it was a gloss of the same thought. One might think it odd that the same thought feels different across languages. This whole mulling over language takes time. Words gather en masse yet they don't tell a story; they just sit there in a pile in her mind ... As the day went on, she thought to herself that there were certainly merits to reviving languages that were almost dead, and to exploring each language for its own sake. This would incite a renewal of philosophy for the service of the future, a philosophy that was often lost in the battles of many languages on one tongue. The truths that populated Qalqalah's mind that day had all been spoken on the tongues of ancient linguists, but none lived long enough to give account.[31]

Dans son état de détresse, elle remarque qu'ielle use de termes anglais pour nommer ses affects. Devrait-ielle user d'une langue avec laquelle ielle n'a pas de relations directes pour rester à distance de ses

émotions ? Ielle se demande en quoi ces mots valent
mieux que ceux de sa langue maternelle.[32]

Is speaking more than one language a form of
treason masked as knowledge?[33]

*

"If words are used to blur things, it is because the battle
over words is inseparable from the battle over things."*[34]
This quote by Jacques Rancière appears as an epigraph in
philosopher Marie-José Mondzain's book *Confiscation des
mots, des usages et du temps* (Confiscation of words, images,
and time).[35] In this thought-provoking essay, Mondzain
denounces the (mis)appropriation of certain words that
are given new, biased definitions and saturate political and
media discourses, thus exhausting sensory capacities and
critical resources. She concentrates her analysis on the
embezzlement of two terms—*radicalité* (radicalism) and
déradicalisation (deradicalization)—by the spokespersons
and policymakers of the French war on terror,[36] in the
very context that prompted the appearance of Qalqalah.

32 Situations Post, et al., "Qalqalah: émoji béton sucré" (2022),
    Qalqalah قلقلة, https://qalqalah.org/fr/histoires/qalqalah
    -4-emoji-beton-sucre.
33 Rifky, "The Subject of Language."
34 Jacques Rancière, *La haine de la démocratie* (Paris: La fabrique
    éditions, 2005).
35 Mondzain, *Confiscation des mots*. The following quotes are
    found on pages 48, 113, and 105.
36 According to Mondzain, radicalization became synonymous
    with the real or phantasmatic exposure of certain commu-
    nities—more or less openly characterized as French citizens

Mondzain vividly criticizes "the confiscation of the idea of radicalism in favor of a belligerent, law-enforcement use that ineluctably associates radicalism with the exercise of terror."* For her, the violence of religious fundamentalism is anything but radical. It pertains to a submissive regime, which opposes itself to another kind of submissive regime: that of the liberal order, based on the deregulation of exchanges and relationships, which presents itself as the only desirable status quo. On the contrary, Mondzain calls for a reinvestment of radicalism as "a figure of the dignity of thought and the freedom to act at the heart of political life."* This requires labor and time, for anyone to reclaim their capacity to exert their critical potential and imagination. According to Mondzain, artists can play a role in mobilizing that imagination, by creating a stage "where the visible and the audible could be shared,"* a "site of indetermination"* and collective agency.

Such an understanding of art and the role of artists was instrumental in the way Victorine Grataloup and I turned to the figure of Qalqalah as a companion and a guide for navigating conflictual political landscapes through the prisms of language and translation. Our interlocution with Qalqalah notably manifested in a group exhibition, "Qalqalah قلقلة: plus d'une langue / More Than One Language," presented at the Centre

---

of immigrant descent living in the suburbs—to Islamic fundamentalism. In turn, deradicalization came to designate measures and programs aiming to *cure* these persons of their radicalization in order to bring them back into the republican, secularist bosom—often through coercion.

régional d'art contemporain Occitanie (CRAC) in Sète and La Kunsthalle in Mulhouse.[37] Featuring works from fourteen artists and collectives, the exhibition coincided with the public launch of the Qalqalah قلقلة online editorial platform in March 2020.[38] The exhibition and the website were conceived together and sought to establish interrelated spaces in which plural stories and heterogeneous accounts could respond to each other while unsettling nationalist, homogenous conceptions of languages. Letters from different alphabets, words, and voices populated the stage of the exhibition—notably thanks to Montasser Drissi's graphic intervention, a dance of quotes, words, letters, and signs spreading across the high walls of the CRAC, around and between the artworks. We wished to generate an immersive experience reminding visitors that languages and discourses are inseparable from speaking and listening bodies, anchored in heterogenous political, historical, and affective realities.

37 The first iteration of the exhibition was presented from March 7 to September 6, 2020, in Sète, the second from February 18 to May 23, 2021, in Mulhouse. Both exhibitions remained closed for several months because of the regulations surrounding the Covid-19 pandemic.

38 The exhibition presented works by Lawrence Abu Hamdan, Sophia Al Maria, Mounira Al Solh, Noureddine Ezarraf, Fehras Publishing Practices, Benoît Grimalt, Wiame Haddad, Vir Andres Hera, institute for incongruous translation (Natascha Sadr Haghighian and Ashkan Sepahvand) with Can Altay, Serena Lee, Scriptings #47: *Man schenkt keinen Hund* (Christine Lemke and Achim Lengerer/Scriptings), Ceel Mogami de Haas, Sara Ouhaddou, Temporary Art Platform (Works on Paper), and a graphic intervention by Montasser Drissi.

Several artworks presented in "Qalqalah قلقلة: plus d'une langue" directly address the affective and political stakes of language through the ambivalent prism of untranslatability. For *Conflicted Phonemes*, artist and forensic listener Lawrence Abu Hamdan collaborated with twelve Somali citizens whose asylum applications had been rejected on the basis of accent analysis conducted over the phones by a private agency.[39] With the help of designer Janna Ulrich, as well as linguists, researchers, activists, and cultural institutions, a series of maps were produced illustrating how accents, dialects, and voices never stop evolving and hybridizing over the course of migratory journeys that sometimes span several years. Presented in both artistic and legal contexts, these maps show that it is not possible to reduce a voice to an identity that is restricted to one space, nationality, or language. They remind us that all acts of listening and translating are inherently political. In court, these maps were used as evidence to undermine the use of accent analysis tests in asylum policies, thus effectively trespassing the boundaries usually ascribed to artworks.

Conflicted Phonemes had been an important trigger and long-term artistic companion in my research on the political implications of translation and untranslatability. This was also the case with another project presented in the exhibition: *Seeing Studies*, convened by Natascha Sadr Haghighian and Ashkan Sepahvand under the name

---

39 Lawrence Abu Hamdan, *Conflicted Phonemes*, 2012;
vinyl wall text, nine A4 sized vinyl prints, and nine stacks
of printed A4 paper.

institute for incongruous translation.[40] Their collaboration takes as its starting point a book published by the Iranian Ministry of Education for teaching art to school children. Based on a seemingly insignificant undertaking—translating that book from Farsi into English—the project reveals how our ways of seeing, describing, representing, and understanding the world are informed by multiple cultural, social, and political prisms. Artists, writers, art historians, and researchers were invited to supplement the original project by creating exercises, images, or texts. These were collected in a bilingual object-book with multiple reading configurations: it can be unbound, shuffled through, and danced around in exhibition settings, where its pages are hung onto three metallic circles installed at different heights in a display conceived by Can Altay. By engaging the body in a spatialized act of reading, with unusual, at times uncomfortable positions while at the same time refusing access to a complete overview of the work, visitors are invited to go through an embodied experience of the situated processes of seeing, learning, and (un)translating that are at the core of *Seeing Studies*.

Untranslatability bears the risk of foreclosing the other altogether—as shown by the collective study of German language books used in "integration courses" for the project *Man schenkt keinen Hund* (We are not offering dogs, 2016);[41] and opens up critical and transformative

40   institute for incongruous translation, *Seeing Studies* (Berlin: Hatje Cantz, 2011).

41   *Man schenkt keinen Hund* was initiated by Christine Lemke in collaboration with Achim Lengerer's publication project Scriptings. This multipart book and exhibition project brings

approaches to language—as in Mounira Al Solh's installation *Sama'/ Ma'as* (2014–17). This monumental work features anagrams of polysemic Arabic words sewn onto both sides of large-scale, colorful textile banners. Circulating around the banners, Arabic speakers are confronted with the disorientation and deceit of multiple interpretations: توت (*tout*: ripe / *tout*: the first month of the Coptic calendar, or the sound of a horn, or a famous song about Beirut); بغر (*raghb*: desire) / رغب (*ghabar*: dust). This work was presented in dialogue with Vir Andres Hera's film *Piramidal* (2016–20), for which the artist transliterated a seventeenth-century poem by Sor Juana Inés de la Cruz into Aljamiado—a coded language used in Andalusia before the Reconquista, which transliterated Spanish texts using the Arabic alphabet. Read aloud by an Algerian individual the artist met on the street as well as by a friend from Saudi Arabia, the poem remains incomprehensible for both Arabic and Spanish speakers, although a sense of uncanny familiarity may arise in the act of listening.

Both artworks invoke a certain visual exuberance: Hera's film displays images from a Catholic procession in Spain, a Baroque spectacle taking us back to the imperial era, while the camera reveals the ambiguity of gender roles and eroticized representations of death in religious performances. Al Solh's installation fills the space with

together writers, activists, artists, course participants, and educators. Conceived as an open-ended research project, *Man schenkt keinen Hund* adopted various approaches and artistic/theoretical/activist strategies to problematize the identarian national discourses around the concept of "integration."

shiny, ornate fabrics that used to populate local markets and decorate domestic interiors in Lebanon before they were mass-produced in other parts of the world. A layered critique of exoticism is thus at play here, which gives new meaning to the frustration one may feel when met with opaque linguistic content. Indeed, both works voluntarily resist and deceive translation and transparency. Although their textual meanings were inaccessible for many of the exhibition's French visitors, they suggested a playful, even subversive relationship to language and how it manifests in public space. Alongside other works in the exhibition, they also enacted a political gesture, by reinscribing Arabic languages and scripts on the walls of a French public institution, in defiance of the negative connotations often imposed onto them in the French context—where proposals to foster the teaching of Arabic language in public schools are regularly accused of fueling so-called communitarianism.[42]

---

42   In a chapter called "L'école publique contre l'arabe" (Public school against Arabic), Nabil Wakim describes the numerous political, ideological, and practical obstacles that obstruct the teaching of Arabic languages in France. He notably recalls the infuriated reactions coming from the right and the far right following different proposals by successive ministers of national education to improve the teaching of Arabic in French public schools, leading to the withdrawal of their projects. Wakim, *L'arabe pour tous: Pourquoi ma langue est taboue en France* (Paris: Éditions du Seuil, 2020), 99–122.

*

In fact, the lexical field of community provided me with my first practical encounter with untranslatability. In several art-related texts I have translated from Englishes, community is charged with positive, emancipatory connotations—in phrases like "community-engaged art," "community-based projects," or "community centers." But over the last two decades in France, the notion of *communauté*, and more specifically the adjective *communautaire*, have progressively been associated with religious (i.e., Islamist) "separatism." *Communautaire* is most frequently used to qualify an "ideology against," a "threat against," or a "drift away from"* so-called French republican values.[43]

During the Qalqalah قلقلة exhibition in Mulhouse, legal expert Hocine Sadok explained to us in a private conversation that, in the case of France, the friction around the notion of community derives from a conception of solidarity as a state monopoly—which notably manifests in the legal implementation of the *délit de solidarité* (solidarity offense). Whenever a group or a community claims alternative forms of solidarity, it is considered a threat to the state/the nation/the republic, especially when these claims stem from "nonwhite persons"—as Afrofeminist

---

[43]   Sylvie Tissot, "Qui a peur du communautarisme ? Réflexions critiques sur une rhétorique réactionnaire," *les mots sont importants*, October 28, 2019, https://lmsi.net/Qui-a-peur-du-communautarisme.

collective Mwasi points out.[44] Indeed, the word "com-munity" has come to encompass and criminalize many different ways of forming communities and of common-ing. In such a case, mobilizing untranslatability does not presuppose an impossibility: it refers to an ethical and political imperative, which demands that words be care-fully examined, contextualized, and reclaimed as they travel across languages.

Against this confiscation and its biopolitical effects, philosopher Nadia Yala Kisukidi chose to reinvest the lexicon of community from a Black feminist perspec-tive. In her beautiful talk "L'hospitalité raciale" (Racial hospitality) she declared that what the French state den-igrates as communitarianism designates, for her, the "concrete dreams of racial hospitality as a refuge."*[45] It is "the production of a community in which, at last, as Baldwin would say, the possibility of inventing oneself, loving oneself and being oneself becomes conceivable."* Kisukidi's talk points to the way community formations are racialized in how they are perceived and evaluated. Yet in France, the word "race" causes so much trouble that

44   "If communitarianism is a rather positive term in the United States, that term possesses a pejorative connotation in France, due to the different discourses and political parties that have opposed it during the past fifteen years. Indeed, communitarianism/separatism is perceived as a threat against republican unity, insomuch as it is invested by nonwhite people."* Mwasi Collectif, *Glossaire*, 2020, https://www .mwasicollectif.org/glossaire/ (last accessed March 12, 2025).

45   Nadia Yala Kisukidi, "L'hospitalité raciale" (lecture, ~~La Colonie~~, Paris, March 29, 2018), audio recording, 16:05, R22 Tout-Monde, https://www.r22.fr/antennes/espace -khiasma/black-lens/l-hospitalite-raciale.

huge efforts are made to erase it from the public sphere:
in 2018, the National Assembly voted to remove it from
the first article of the French Constitution, which defines
the republic's founding values.[46] Activists and scholars
who insist on using it to denounce racism or retrace its
history are often accused of fueling racism in turn, in what
Achille Mbembe has called "a spectacular turnaround."*[47]
As sociologist Sarah Mazouz observes: "Reasserting the
need to resort critically to the concept of race could be
used to emerge from that paradox of an abstract univer-
salism, which actually individualizes and disqualifies what
is conceived as heterogenous to the social body."*[48]

*

Many of these contested terms indeed have to do with
delineating the contours of "French republican values,"

[46] Instead of ensuring that "all citizens are equal in front of the
      law, without distinction of origin, race or religion,"* the
      revised article states that France "ensures that all citizens are
      equal in front of the law, without distinction of sex, origin,
      or religion."*

[47] Achille Mbembé recently argued that "in the West, as well
      as in other parts of the world, we are witnessing the rise
      of new forms of racism that could be qualified as paroxysmal.
      Paroxysmal racism has the particularity that it metabolically
      infiltrates the operations of power, technology, culture,
      language, and even the atmosphere we breathe. [...] But
      the virulence of contemporary racism can only be equaled
      by its denial. [...] In a spectacular turnaround, anti-racist
      struggles are being held responsible for the rise of racism."*
      Achille Mbembe, "Notes sur l'eurocentrisme tardif," *AOC*,
      March 16, 2021, https://aoc.media/analyse/2021/03/16
      /notes-sur-leurocentrisme-tardif/.

[48] Sarah Mazouz, *Race* (Paris: Anamosa, 2020), 82.

in opposition to so-called separatist forces.[49] In French political and public discourse, the deafening prevalence of terms such as separatism or communitarianism naturalizes the boundary between a fictitious "us" and a fantasized "them," the latter often being pictured as a racialized Other (even when they hold French citizenship). This type of discourse produces a reconfiguration of language and vocabularies, which crystallizes most aggressively into exacerbated anti-Muslim positions and actions at the state level and in all strata of society. Activists, scholars, nonprofits, and individuals who denounce the rise of Islamophobia, or who simply call for addressing racial and postcolonial realities in France (whether in the academic context or in society at large) have openly been accused of fueling the division of the republic and encouraging terrorism.[50] This impossible

[49] On October 2, 2020, Emmanuel Macron delivered a speech on the fight against separatisms (in the plural), which exclusively targeted Islamic separatism. The speech also denounced, once again, the role of "certain theories of social sciences completely imported from the United States" in fueling "ideological and exclusively political debates."* Macron, "La République en actes: Discours du Président de République sur le theme de la lutte contre les séparatismes," October 2, 2020, https://www.elysee.fr /emmanuel-macron/2020/10/02/la-republique-en -actes-discours-du-president-de-la-republique-sur-le -theme-de-la-lutte-contre-les-separatismes.

[50] On October 31, 2020, ninety prominent French intellectuals and academics published a statement in *Le Monde*, supporting Minister of National Education Jean-Michel Blanquer's allegations that "very powerful Islamo-leftists trends in the sectors of higher education are doing great harm" and that the murder of school teacher Samuel Paty was "conditioned by people who encourage such intellectual radicalism."*

dialogue found a striking expression in the much debated accusation of "Islamo-leftism," a term that dominated political discourse in 2020–21. Denounced as baseless by the individuals, institutions, and movements it targets, it nevertheless had concrete and dangerous effects: from the defunding of research programs to the dissolution of non-profits, and the public shaming and private harassment of academics and activists, to name a few.[51]

This antagonistic field led Qalqalah قلقلة to invite Houda Asal to retrace the history of the terms Islamophobia and separatism, and their circulations in

They denounced the "indigenist, radicalist, and 'decolonial' ideologies (transferred from North American campuses), which nurture the hatred of 'Whites' and of France, and violent activism."* "Une centaine d'universitaires alertent: 'Sur l'islamisme, ce qui nous menace, c'est la persistance du déni,'" *Le Monde*, October 31, 2020, https://www.lemonde.fr/idees/article/2020/10/31/une-centaine-d-universitaires-alertent-sur-l-islamisme-ce-qui-nous-menace-c-est-la-persistance-du-deni_6057989_3232.html.

51   On March 20, 2021, international academics expressed solidarity with their French peers, who were targeted by a call from Frédérique Vidal (Minister of Higher Education, Research and Innovation) to launch a public investigation against "Islamo-leftism" and its "gangrene" in French academia. They declared: "The relatively new term 'Islamo-gauchisme' reflects a much older convergence of right-wing, colonial and racist ideologies working in opposition to anti-colonial, anti-Islamophobia [sic] and anti-racism struggles." "International Statement of Solidarity with Decolonial Academics and Activists in France," *Informed Comment,* March 20, 2021, https://www.juancole.com/2021/03/international-solidarity-decolonial.html.

French and international discourses.[52] In her text, written
in French and translated into English and Arabic, Asal
examines the way these specific terms historically trav-
eled across languages and countries, taking a stand against
their biased use in the French context. As she declares
in her introduction: "It is in fact urgent to reappropri-
ate the terms of the debate as it is imposed in France,
with its vacuous terminology, racist logic and perpet-
ual blackmail." Such work, for her, demands a refusal of
the neutrality that is still often required from researchers,
particularly "racialized researchers working on racism."
Although I cannot claim to speak from a similar position, since I am not a racialized researcher, Asal's refusal
of neutrality offers a guiding principle for approaching
the labor of translation and editing, and sharing the work
of reappropriation that she calls for. I also recognize this
call in the work of several collectives who are reclaiming
the academic forms of glossaries and lexicons as critical,
political tools.

*

In the foreword to their *Petit lexique en voie de décolonisation* (Little lexicon on the way to decolonization), Collectif

52   Asal, "From Islamophobia to Separatism." This invitation
      followed an online public conversation, organized by
      Qalqalah قلقلة together with Hostile Environment(s) in May
      2021, during which Asal, scholar Sara R. Farris, and curator
      Edwin Nasr discussed the interrelations of femonationalism
      and Islamophobia in France and Europe. A recording
      of the conversation is available at https://qalqalah.org/en
      /activities/conversation-in-the-name-of.

Piment (comprised of writers and music producers Célia Potiron, Christiano Soglo, Binetou Sylla, and Rhoda Tchokokam) observes that dictionaries hold the power to define concepts without situating the so-called expertise of their authors and lexicographers. Analyzing the reductive, pacifying definition of "racism" in the Larousse dictionary, they note how such official definitions often take precedence over the voices of those who actually suffer from, investigate, or fight against racism. Instead, they propose "to redirect the gaze from the margins, inscribing [them]selves within a tradition of Black sousveillance"*—a concept forged by scholar Simone Browne, which calls for hijacking the tools of social control to fight against anti-Black surveillance. Collectif Piment deliberately chose the form of a lexicon—albeit an eminently subjective and heterogenous one, where humor and literary experimentation hold a prominent place. It allowed them to "index old and new words, follow the evolution of certain definitions and languages, coming out of a decade that [they] consider decisive for the future of Black populations in France. The lexicon is a tool to reflect on and think about [their] place in society, [their] relationship to it and to [them]selves."*[53]

Afrofeminist activist collective Mwasi, formed in 2014, also chose to publish an online glossary as part of their political struggle against a racist, heteropatriarchal, and capitalist system. The glossary includes a selection of terms stemming from critical race theory, gender studies,

---

53   Collectif Piment, *Le dérangeur. Petit lexique en voie de décolonisation* (Marseille: Hors d'atteinte, 2020), 16.

and bottom-up militant work. It inscribes these terms into a global reflection and struggle while detailing their implications specific to the French context. The definitions are rather short and straightforward, yet they are historically and theoretically situated, so that they could be used as political arguments. In their introduction, Mwasi state: "Words are important; they dredge relations of domination and serve as a way to apprehend the real, but they also indicate our political objectives and strategies. We wish to make accessible here concepts that we use as part of our struggles, so that, our sisters and brothers could use them, question, criticize and enrich them."*[54] *Les mots sont importants* (Words are important) is also the name of a website, founded in the 2000s by a collective of scholars to analyze the way mainstream media perpetuates a political use of language that euphemizes and legitimates state violence to the detriment of the most precarious parts of the population—whose speech is in turn regularly discredited.[55]

These examples show how activists and scholars are reclaiming the codes of lexicons and glossaries in order to intervene in the "battle over words" by collectively forging critical tools that are made easily accessible via online platforms. Such work implies that the co-authors acknowledge their situated positions and their heterogenous engagement with language(s)—as I experienced myself during the collective elaboration of a multilingual lexicon on love and prejudice, as part of a collaboration

54   Mwasi Colectif, *Glossaire*.
55   See https://lmsi.net/.

between Qalqalah قلقلة, artist Mounira Al Solh, and international students from the program Exerce – Masters of Choreography, in Montpellier. During a three-day workshop in November 2020, we collectively assembled a series of words, in various languages, which either crystallized relations of power and experiences of prejudice, or feelings of tenderness, desire, and care. Subjective definitions were written in order to reclaim those words, defuse their toxicity, or enhance their affective power. Later, we performed these recharged words for each other, addressing them to each other like gifts, or antidotes.[56]

In 2023, Salma Mochtari and myself also composed a "disoriented glossary" as part of a yearlong project called "Enough History / كفانا حكايا / Ne me raconte plus d'Histoire," developed through Qalqalah قلقلة's research affiliation with Tanzquartier Wien. Based on our conversations with philosopher Ariella Aïsha Azoulay, artist Mohamed Abdelkarim, and participants in a series of workshops, we revisited words and expressions such as "archive," "fiction," "embodied communities," "gestures of unlearning," "refusing neutrality," and "strike."[57] Collectively elaborating these counter-glossaries became a method, which we regularly redeployed and actualized in response to various contexts. Each glossary displays one possible, temporary set of meanings, open to contestation and reimagination. They are conceived as writing

---

56 Some of our glossaries were published on https://qalqalah.org/.

57 See Salma Mochtari and Virginie Bobin, "Notes on Enough History: A Disoriented Glossary" (2023), Qalqalah قلقلة, https://qalqalah.org/en/notes-on-enough-history -a-disoriented-glossary.

forms in themselves, modes of storytelling, suggesting once more a troubled relationship to the contingent truths that words carry along.

*

In her book *Le pouvoir des mots* (The power of words), sociolinguist Josiane Boutet examines how the symbolic appropriation of words plays a crucial role in political struggle.[58] She analyses various linguistic strategies and countertactics throughout the twentieth century to today (i.e., naming, renaming, misuse, or wordplay) that seek to sustain or counteract the dissemination of what she compares to "earworms": ready-made political expressions born out of a technocratic conception of language that aims to govern bodies by means of linguistic manipulation and viral dissemination. In a chapter called "Rétablir la vérité. Critiquer les mots" (Restoring the truth: Criticizing words), Boutet refers to another opponent of the Nazi regime, Bertold Brecht, who called for restoring the real meaning of words through a detailed process of deconstruction and translation. Considering it an intellectual duty and a political action, Brecht set out to "clean" the words soiled by Nazi rhetoric. To do so, he *restored* Nazi political speeches, reformulating them to reveal the power relations of exploitation and control disguised under a rhetoric of unity and fervor. In French, the word *rétablissement* (reinstatement, restoration, recovery), which was used by Brecht's translators Paul Dehem and

58   Josiane Boutet, *Le pouvoir des mots* (Paris: La Dispute, 2016).

Philippe Ivernel to describe this operation, is associated with the restoration of truth as well as with healing of the body. It postulates that language has been sickened by the very agents who claim to be the proponents of linguistic or national integrity, thus infecting locutors with deformed truths that serve to mask concrete political violence.

When it comes to language and translation, the recurrence of sanitary or medical metaphors is striking. Conservative, identarian understandings of language, culture, or nation often compare them to (female) bodies whose integrity must be protected. For researcher Myriam Suchet, the dominant representations of language often rely on what she calls "the immune paradigm"—riffing on Roberto Esposito's work on the correlation between the development of immunology and the political representations of national communities based on protectionism.[59] In a two-part essay titled "Démasquer 'la langue,' ce virus" (Unmasking "the language," this virus), written for Qalqalah قلقلة's *Research diaries* in 2020, Suchet interrogates the effects of the political and sanitary responses to the Covid-19 pandemic on the representations of "language."[60] She notes the rapid emergence of a new lexicon in response to this extraordinary situation, built upon a series of neologisms as well as on the attribution of new meanings to existing words, which in turn shaped social

---

59   Roberto Esposito, *Terms of the Political: Community, Immunity, Biopolitics*, trans. Rhiannon Noel Welch (New York: Fordham University Press, 2008).

60   Myriam Suchet, "Démasquer la langue, ce virus 1/2" (2020), Qalqalah قلقلة, https://qalqalah.org/fr/carnets-de-recherche/demasquer-la-langue-ce-virus-1.

practices. The widespread use of *gestes barrières* (barrier gestures), for example, propagated an imaginary of (self-) protection, separation, and mutual exclusion. Wondering how to reverse that linguistic order, Suchet asks how our attraction to new words might be converted into an emancipatory potential and a political struggle. She turns to William Burroughs's conception of the word as a virus, set to invade and corrupt western languages; to resist and to survive "at [their] expense."[61]

To restore, to heal, to resist, and to survive. These verbs bring to mind Donna Haraway's notion of recuperation, which she favors over restoration or reconciliation: a fragile, incomplete way of forming alliances and "staying with the trouble." Here again, the polysemy of the verb *récupérer* (i.e., retrieving, rehabilitating, salvaging, recycling, saving, collecting, catching one's breath, recovering) opens up a wide array of potential ways of doing with words and with others. Although recuperation exceeds, for Haraway, human languages and traditional understandings of translation, it also belongs to the realm of storytelling, of fabulation and speculation. It implies to be "enmeshed in partial and flawed translations across difference"[62]—not to erase them but to *consider* them. It suggests an embodied, affected engagement that transforms the translatress and her companions in the process.

*

61　　William Burroughs, *Electronic Revolution* [1970] (New York: Ubu Classics, 2005).

62　　Haraway, *Staying with the Trouble*, 10.

In the aforementioned essay, Myriam Suchet carefully inscribes her reflections into an embodied conception of language as a social and political practice. For example, how does the obligation to wear protective masks impede the possibility of engaging with others in the frame of a FFL (French as a Foreign Language)[63] class? The textile barrier, which dissimulates the mouth and muffles the voice, effectively alters mutual transmission by limiting it to linguistic content—to the detriment of the vocal intonations, lip-reading, and facial expressions that play such an important role in dialogical and learning exchanges. Masks become a crude reminder of the multiple obstacles faced by those whose right to survival is partly conditioned upon the acquisition of French language.[64]

Alexandra Galitzine-Loumpet and Marie-Caroline Saglio-Yatzimirsky, coordinators of the research program LIMINAL (Linguistic and Intercultural Mediations in a context of International Migrations), also denounced the violent inequalities enforced by the management of the pandemic in France, which increased the vulnerability of exiled persons living in overcrowded centers or facing

---

63 In a subsequent text published on qalqalah.org, Suchet proposed to twist the acronym FLE into *français langue étrangée* (French as a foreign*ed* language) as a way of troubling language, its representations and its political manifestations. Myriam Suchet, "Une lettre en *français langue étrangée*" (2021), Qalqalah قلقلة, https://qalqalah.org/fr/carnets-de-recherche /une-lettre-en-francais-langue-etrangee.

64 Not only on a practical basis, but also on a legal one: each person applying for a residential permit in France must take a French language exam as part of a *contrat d'intégration républicaine* (contract of republican integration).

the dismantling of their makeshift camps.[65] For them, such inequalities also manifest in the lack of translation resources provided to exiled persons who face an exclusively Francophone bureaucratic machine—despite the fact that they have a legal right to translation. If this situation existed before the pandemic, these "translation deficits"* effectively prevented people from accessing information about safety measures, healthcare and Covid-related regulations. This exposed them not only to higher sanitary risks, but also to increased police controls and to the threat of deportation. Consciously hijacking the state's rhetoric, LIMINAL called for a "translation state of emergency"*—not as a temporary, circumstantial response to a given crisis, but as a sustainable set of actions acknowledging the constant urgency of providing proper conditions for the reception of those seeking better living conditions.

If the linguistic violence enacted by the lack of translation produces silence and exclusion, it also generates lexical inventions and countertactics that contribute to alter dominant representations and open performative interstices. Between 2016 and 2021, LIMINAL researchers collected a series of words used at borders, reception centers, and other places of transit by those affected by, or involved in, asylum procedures. A database of more

---

65 Marie-Caroline Saglio Yatzimirsky and Alexandra Galitzine-Loumpet, "Covid-19 et au-delà: Pourquoi la question des langues est vitale en migration," *Azil* (blog), *Mediapart*, May 27, 2020, https://blogs.mediapart.fr/liminal/blog /270520/covid-19-et-au-dela-pourquoi-la-question-des -langues-est-vitale-en-migration.

than 2,000 words was published in five languages (Arabic, Farsi, Pashto, Urdu, and Tigrinya) on a website called MIGRalect, mapping how "language practices in situations of migration are made of violence and imposition but also borrowing, embezzlement, and creativity."[66] These words, transiting across multiple tongues, manifest the permanent processes of makeshift translation and creation, as well as the confrontations and tenuous negotiations at play between the languages of administrations, nonprofits, and exiled persons. MIGRalect also invites French readers to pay attention to the representations that these neologisms vehiculate and what they have to say about their own institutions and policies. In doing so, it proposes to reconfigure the positions of the utterer and the uttered: of those who have the power to name, enunciate, and describe, and those who must compose with the disorienting reality forged by the words of others.

*

The various examples above are another way to remind us that "word battles" are notably grounded in the refusal (on the part of most politicians, the conservative press, and some academics) to address the ongoing relation between France's colonial history and its racially organized present—blindly clinging to imaginary universal values that serve to exclude any person, collective, or fantasized category that resists assimilating (to) them. In "Colonial Aphasia: Disabled Histories and Race in

France," a chapter from her book *Duress*, historian Ann Laura Stoler criticizes the recurrent recourse to a so-called "colonial amnesia" in order to describe the general elision of colonial history in the French public discourse, in parallel with a recent surge of historical projects addressing that very history since the turn of the twenty-first century.[67] According to her, this history "may be displaced, occluded from view, or rendered inappropriate to pursue. *It may be difficult to retrieve in a language* that speaks to the disparate violence it engendered. But it is neither forgotten nor absent from contemporary life."

Stoler's focus on language is important, as she proposes to name this phenomenon "colonial aphasia," a term that accurately renders the idea of an impediment as well as a feeling of loss. Aphasia, for Stoler, "is a dismembering, a difficulty in speaking, a difficulty in generating a vocabulary that associates appropriate words and concepts to appropriate things. [It] describes a difficulty in retrieving both conceptual and lexical vocabularies and, most important, a difficulty in comprehending what is spoken." What should matter, to Stoler, is how these dis(re)membered stories participate in the way partitions and exclusions are systematically established in contemporary politics, and how they reverberate in "the grammar of Republican values."

Reading or producing counter-glossaries, unfolding the contested meanings of words and the conflicting

---

67   Ann Laura Stoler, *Duress: Imperial Durabilities in Our Times* (Durham, NC: Duke University Press, 2016), 127–30 and 167 (my emphasis).

agendas of their users, cannot be compared to the kind of historical work described by Stoler. It should not pretend to be an act of decolonization, even metaphorically—as Eve Tuck and K. Wayne Yang would argue.[68] It could nevertheless be approached as an attempt to confront colonial aphasia, both about the past and in/for the present. For colonial aphasia is also my legacy, as a white French citizen born in the 1980s—a decade marked both by the rise of the Front National and the surge of anti-racist movements. French colonial histories were absent from family discussions in my childhood, although my grandparents lived through the Indochina and Algerian wars. They were only mentioned in passing in school programs that often withheld their violence. École du Louvre, where I studied art history and museum studies in the early 2000s, managed the tour de force of teaching students about the production of objects and artworks from all eras and geographic areas while barely reflecting on the geopolitical dimensions that shaped the world of their makers—and later brought them to French museums. It was only outside of the familial and French educational frameworks that I was later able to unlearn, with companions, the way certain

68   Eve Tuck and K. Wayne Yang remind us that decolonization differs from social justice projects and should not be confused with the establishment of critical methodologies and curriculums in schools and universities. In the context in which they write, that of settler colonialism, decolonization "must involve the repatriation of land simultaneous to the recognition of how land and relations to land have always already been differently understood and enacted." Tuck and Yang, "Decolonization Is Not a Metaphor," *Decolonization: Indigeneity, Education & Society* 1, no. 1 (2012): 1–40.

stories were told to me, and to acknowledge how other stories were silenced or warped, with long-lasting effects into the present.[69]

Stoler concludes her chapter with the following call: "We need a better understanding of how inaccessibility to knowledge is achieved and more about the political, scholarly, and cognitive domains in which knowing is disabled, attention is redirected, things are renamed, and disregard is revived and sustained. At issue is both disabled knowledge as a political form and 'knowing' as a cognitive and affective act." I believe that collective endeavors to scrutinize and engage in the "battle over words" can contribute to such better understanding, and restore meaning from aphasic fragments. By carefully tending to untranslatability, ongoing gestures of translation can play a significant role in this effort. Indeed, they necessitate an active engagement with critical discourses and heterogenous positions stemming from different contexts and experiences. They facilitate the decentering of positions and views, maintaining unstable perspectives on the linguistic and political "territory in which [we] maneuver." That labor does not aim at a resolution, and it should not be idealized or romanticized. It is just an ethical invitation

---

69 Ariella Aïsha Azoulay writes: "Unlearning with companions means no longer privileging the accounts of imperial agents, scholars included, and instead retrieving other modalities of sharing the world and the many refusals inherent in people's public performances, diverse claims, and repressed aspirations." Azoulay, *Potential History: Unlearning Imperialism* (London: Verso, 2019), 16.

to constantly negotiate with the equivocality among the words and narratives that they sustain or trouble.

Unlearning with Others

Resisting from the Inside:
Imperial Languages, Plural Voices

In 2017, I began collaborating with artist Mercedes Azpilicueta around her evolving project *Bestiario de Lengüitas*, which follows the thread of a script written for a future performance that may never happen. Over the course of four years, a series of workshops, collaborations, and rehearsals with artists, researchers, designers, dancers, and singers were organized, culminating in three exhibitions and a publication.[70] Filled with obsolete knowledge systems, *neobarroso* poems, failed translations, and ambiguous ingredients, Mercedes's[71] script hosts a choir of grotesque characters who loudly struggle to maintain chaos and excess in a world calling for order, efficiency, and transparency. Living or dead; existing or fictive; humans, protheses, animals, demons, or plants— they converse in a polyphony of languages and voices that obfuscate straightforward narratives.

70   This collaboration began during Azpilicueta's Pernod Ricard Fellowship residency at Villa Vassilieff in Paris, where I used to work as head of programs. It has included public workshops at Villa Vassilieff and Cité des Arts (Paris) and CentroCentro (Madrid); three exhibitions that I curated, at CentroCentro, Museion (Bolzano), and CAC Brétigny, between 2019 and 2021; a podcast on *Duuu Radio in 2021; various texts; and a book published by K. Verlag in 2024.

71   Although it goes against academic conventions, I sometimes use my research companions' first names (after introducing their full name in the text) to acknowledge the intimate relationships and bonds that sustain our collaborations.

Language and the spoken word are central elements of Mercedes's practice. In her performance *Yegua-yeta-yuta* (2015–ongoing), she regurgitates a litany of insults commonly directed at women in Argentina—engaging her voice, her body, and her breath into a kind of collective exorcism. Her work strives to articulate minorized, delegitimized positions, while embracing opacity and experimenting with the dislocation of language and its sexist, racist violence. Working together and building friendship across five languages and three countries, our relationship was enmeshed in constant acts of translation—between languages, media, and contexts—that nurtured and transformed our respective practices. It opened porous circulations between the seemingly established roles of researcher, author, artist, *curatrice*, and translatress. It welcomed the precarious joy of collective constructions—always shaky and incomplete—unfolding through interlaced economies of production, attention, and friendship.

For the third iteration of the exhibition "Bestiario de Lengüitas," which took place at CAC Brétigny, an art center located in the Paris *banlieue*, Mercedes, the team, and I decided to produce a sound piece based on a French version of the script. The text would be interpreted by comedian Emmanuelle Lafon, who had already performed preliminary versions of the script across three languages for the videos presented in the exhibition. Researcher Annabella Tournon was commissioned to translate the Spanish original into French, in addition to the French version of the prologue that I had previously translated. Both texts were carefully edited in close conversation with Annabella, Mercedes, and Emmanuelle. Indeed, a new parameter of translation entered into play, as the text was to be read aloud. Thus, the choice of words and their placement in sentences were also determined by their *mise en bouche*, their taste, their rhythm, and their sound. We had to translate "with our feet," remembering writer, curator, and translator Omar Berrada's advice:

> You break a text apart to let it enter through the pores of your body, to get a sense of its cadence. This takes time. [...] To imbue yourself with its rhythm, let it run through your body. It is with your body that you translate, not with your mind. You don't need to understand the words of the text as much as you need to dance to its rhythms. Why do you think poetry has feet? Use yours when you translate.[72]

A discussion occurred with Emmanuelle about the use of "inclusive" writing in the prologue and the script.[73] "Inclusive" language has been notoriously difficult to adapt to spoken French—as its opponents repeatedly point out. It grates and grinds through the teeth, it draws out and weighs on the tongue, as it usually manifests

72   Omar Berrada, "Translucination" (lecture, 7th Global Art Forum, Mathaf: Arab Museum of Modern Art, Doha, March 16, 2023), https://www.artdubai.ae/global-art -forum-07/ (recording no longer available as of April 15, 2025).

73   "Inclusive" writing or language is one possible name for a variety of gestures and practices that seek to deconstruct the domination of the masculine subject and binary norms in language. Several feminist authors, such as Julie Abbou, reject this denomination, which for them reflects a normalizing, neutralizing approach based on a neoliberal, universal notion of inclusion. For this reason, I refer to it in quotation marks.

orally through repetition or extension—i.e., *les étudiantes et étudiants, les travailleureuses de l'art*. Emmanuelle wondered how "inclusive" language would trouble her reading, diminishing the fluidity of the spoken text. Take the following passage from the prologue, and try to read the French version aloud:

> Ces poèmes offrent des mots à ma tribu [...]: artistes femmes et queer, enseignant·e·s, grand-mères, syndicalistes, soignant·e·s, tantes, mères, amant·e·s, thérapeuthes, sœurs, filles, migrant·e·s, ami·e·s, marraines, épouses, compagnes, demi-sœurs, chercheur~euses, voyageur~euses, pères absents, cousin·e·s d'adoption, ex-petit·e·s ami·e·s et apprenti·e·s perpétuel·le·s.[74]

We decided to approach the graphic manifestations (such as middle dots) of "inclusive" writing as a score, to exaggerate and amplify them orally. After all, *Bestiario de Lengüitas* also deals with fatigue, indigestion, and sickness. It shelters dissident bodies that refuse to conform to binary norms, even at the risk of death. In her book *Ce que le sida m'a fait* (What AIDS has done to me), art critic Élisabeth Lebovici establishes a parallel between an inventive, nonbinary use of language and the necessity

---

74　"These poems are words for my clan [...]: women and queer artists, professors, grandmothers, union workers, healers, aunts, mothers, lovers, therapists, sisters, daughters, migrants, friends, godmothers, wives, partners, stepsisters, scholars, travelers, absent parents, adoptive cousins, ex-girlfriends, and lifelong learners." Mercedes Azpilicueta, *Bestiary of Tonguelets* (Berlin: K. Verlag, 2024), 45.

of "deviating, distorting and thus widening the range of genders and orientations, which language could gift to sexuation."* The author then asks: "Instead of correcting nonconforming persons to one of the terms of binarity through mutilating procedures [...] why not extend our lexicon?"*[75] How could such a nonbinary, nonconformist way of doing with language be made audible in turn? We opted for chewing the words, letting them fill our mouths and work through our tongues, taking space, making noise, embracing exaggeration, repetition, and discomfort. In the end, Emmanuelle's reading sparked with joy and invention. Her declamation of "*bourgeôâ-âZeuh,*" "*enseignan-anTeuh,*" emphasized the humorous, irreverent quality of the text and turned it into a riotous sonic experience.[76]

*

In French, *écriture inclusive* designates modes of expression that contest the masculine default via different tactics (i.e., feminization, double flexion, or middle dot), thereby shedding light on the ideological foundations of

75 Élisabeth Lebovici, *Ce que le sida m'a fait* (Geneva: JRP|Ringier, 2021), 16.
76 Extracts from the sound piece can be heard in the podcast "Lenguas vivas / langues vivantes / living tongues," which we recorded with Emmanuelle Lafon, Hélène Harder, Lucile Sauzet, Pau Simon, and Myriam Suchet in spring 2021, while the exhibition remained closed to the public because of Covid-related governmental measures. "Lenguas vivas / langues vivantes / living tongues," audio recording, 130:07 min., *Duuu Radio*, March 14, 2021, https://duuuradio .fr/archive/lenguas-vivas-langues-vivantes-living-tongues.

language that are reflected in acts of naming and gender-marking—namely, the maintenance of a heteropatriarchal organization of society to the detriment of women and sexual minorities. Since it was initially carried by feminist and queer activists before spreading to more mainstream channels, "inclusive" writing stirred a moral panic among conservative and liberal voices alike and is continuously brandished as a red flag supposedly marking the decline of French civilization.[77] In her book *Tenir sa langue*, subtitled *Le langage, lieu de lutte féministe* (Holding one's tongue: Language as a site of feminist struggle), Julie Abbou analyzes the ideological intersections of language, gender, and nation in contemporary French republicanism, which considers French language as a vector of national unity. From this perspective, "touching the linguistic gender means touching the nation."[78]

In her short manual *Le langage inclusif: Pourquoi, comment* (Inclusive language: Why, how), literary scholar Éliane Viennot retraces the masculinization of the French

77 In 2017 Académie française published a hilarious "statement on so-called 'inclusive' writing," which "unanimously raise[d] a solemn warning"*: "The multiplication of orthographic and syntactic marks that it induces leads to a language which expression is divided and disparate, thus generating a confusion that borders on illegibility. [...] On this occasion, it is less as a guardian of the norm than as a guarantor for the future that [the academy] sets alarm bells ringing: facing this 'inclusive' aberration, the French language is henceforth in deadly peril."* Académie française, "Déclaration sur l'écriture dite 'inclusive,'" October 26, 2017, https://www.academie-francaise.fr/actualites/declaration-de-lacademie-francaise-sur-lecriture-dite-inclusive.

78 Julie Abbou, *Tenir sa langue. Le langage, lieu de lutte féministe* (Paris: Éditions Les Pérégrines, 2022), 202.

language, which accelerated with the creation of universities in the thirteenth century, printing in the fifteenth century, and the Académie française in the seventeenth century. This process reflected the solidification of gendered hierarchies in a patriarchal society, wherein women were gradually prevented from certain jobs and functions, the names for which then became exclusively masculine. For Viennot, the emergence of "inclusive" language in turn reflects another social evolution, to a more egalitarian society in the making (or, at least, in the naming)—at a time when gender-based discrimination and sexual violence are ardently debated in the public sphere. Far from polarizing, it represents "just a way of caring about expressing oneself in a more accurate and egalitarian manner, by resorting mainly to the traditional resources of the French language, and otherwise to innovations that are currently being elaborated."*[79]

"Inclusive" language is often accused of in fact excluding people who may not have the fluency, education, or physical ability to read, write, and speak that experimental language—thus touching on issues of racism, classism, and ableism. However, this argument has in turn been refuted by some who seek to foster "inclusion" in all its possible forms and put the patriarchal linguistic order to an end. With these important debates in mind, "inclusive" writing is also a fruitful, self-reflexive tool when applied to the translation of English texts. Although gender issues are far less visible in the English

---

79 Éliane Viennot, *Le langage inclusif: Pourquoi, comment* (Donnemarie-Dontilly: Éditions iXe, 2018), 11.

language—which has no grammatical gender—it is still marked by metaphorical gendering and sexism, as translation productively reveals.[80] In *Gender in Translation*, Sherry Simon analyzes the work of several feminist translatresses who, in the last decade of the twentieth century, openly manipulated their English source texts in order to assert their presence as well as to reflect gender struggles. For example, Suzanne de Lotbinière-Harwood called for a "resexing" of the English language, in order to "make the feminine visible in language so that women are seen and heard in the world."[81] Quebecois feminist editor and translatress Barbara Godard described her practice of translation as a way of "womanhandling" the text, thus replacing "the modest, self-effacing translator" with the "feminist translator, affirming her critical difference," who "flaunts the signs of her manipulation of the text."[82]

80   In an essay published just as I was finishing this text, Lebogang Mokoena reminds the readers that "while some languages across the world operate within a cis-heteronormative system (excluding humans who do not define or categorise themselves as either women or men), it is not alien for some people in some cultures to speak languages that are constructed outside of a gender binary." Mokoena, "A Beautiful Mess: Moving Towards Non-Binary Language," *La Revue* (CAC Brétigny), November 30, 2023, https://www.cacbretigny.com/en/847-a-beautiful-mess-moving-towards-non-binary-language.

81   Suzanne de Lotbinière-Harwood, "Geographies of Why," in *Culture in Transit: Translating the Literature of Quebec*, ed. Sherry Simon (Montreal: Véhicule Press, 1995); quoted in Simon, *Gender in Translation*.

82   Barbara Godard, "Theorizing Feminist Theory/Translation," in *Translation: History and Culture*, ed. Susan Bassnett and André Lefevere (London: Frances Pinter, 1990), quoted in Simon, *Gender in Translation*.

However, the calls for a feminization of language at times risk reinstating the very same binarism that these feminist translatresses and writers wished to dismantle in the first place. Such a critique was recently addressed to certain forms of "inclusive" writing that, in using the middle dot to signal the gendered variability of a word (*les travailleur·euse·s internationaux·nales de l'art sont mobilisé·e·s* for "international art workers are mobilizing"), actually emphasize the distinction between the masculine and feminine; and confirm their domination as the two poles through which to read the world. Over the past few years, attempts have been made by marketing agencies to standardize and sell "inclusive" writing, thus defusing its power to mess with the established linguistic order. Although standardization may contribute to greater accessibility—as argued by people with visual or reading impairments, for example—it should not be at the service of a neutralizing, neoliberal worldview.

In *Sur les bouts de la langue*, translatress Noémie Grunenwald writes: "To translate as feminist/s means fighting against the violence exerted by the dominant over the speech of the oppressed. Refusing to take part in its erasure and its instrumentalization by acknowledging our strengths and our limits. It means resisting within language, relying on our comradeships, sororities, loves, connivances, our political and affective bonds."*[83] In a chapter titled *Inclure?* (Including?) she reflects on various ways of using "inclusive" writing in her translations, which echoed my own practical experiences as a

83 Grunenwald, *Sur les bouts de la langue*, 138.

translatress. From that perspective, "inclusive" writing is both a linguistic and political intervention into the aforementioned "word battles" that foregrounds voices other than the dominant masculine one in French, and it disputes the so-called neutrality of translation, by calling attention to the role of the translatress.

Grunenwald remarks that, in collective translation workshops, participants often sought to harmonize the "demasculinization process," by giving preeminence to one style of "inclusive" writing over the different possibilities initially proposed by the co-translatoresses. As if a rigorous unity of style would enhance the linguistic legitimacy and the political efficiency of that struggle in language. On the contrary, Grunenwald speaks in favor of adapting the use of "inclusive" writing according to each text and each sentence, even if the choices may sound incoherent or contradictory. She encourages us to play it by ear, so to speak, and to have fun with it. For her, experimentation is more fruitful than standardization, and "a hasty regularization would harm the incredible creativity of liberation movements in general—lesbian and feminist ones in particular."* Such a commitment, it is to be noted, often requires negotiating with editors and publishers who regularly seek to standardize "inclusive" writing in the publishing phase of an article or a book—even feminist ones.

Linguist Julie Abbou goes even further, advocating for the use of "disruption, disorder, tumult, and eccentricity"* to emancipate ourselves from and through grammar as a political practice.[84] In my experience,

84 Abbou, *Tenir sa langue*, 212.

this emancipation was also possible thanks to encounters with creative writing and translations by the queer and feminist poets, authors, and artists experimenting with the possibilities of "inclusive" writing in the French language, as well as the work of queer feminist graphic designers—such as the French Belgian collective Bye Bye Binary—who are pushing these possibilities even further by inventing and circulating typographic representations for it.[85] Because they employ graphic interventions, these translation choices are some of the most visible manifestations of the translatress taking a *position* within the text.

*

As Mercedes was just beginning to write the script for *Bestiario de Lengüitas* in Paris, we organized together a series of "dirty translation" workshops at the Cité Internationale des Arts, a large-scale residency space hosting 300 international artists. Mercedes brought fragments from her own texts, as well as a poem by Argentinian writer and activist Néstor Perlongher (1949–1992). Titled "Cadáveres," it was written on Perlongher's way to exile in Brazil in 1981, after he had been detained for his active participation in the Argentinian Homosexual

---

85   Bye Bye Binary introduces itself as "a French Belgian collective, a pedagogical experimentation, a community, a variable typo·graphic workshop, a network, an alliance," which "proposes to explore new graphic and typographic forms adapted to French language [...] taking inclusive and non-binary language and writing as starting point, field of experimentation and research subject."* See https://genderfluid.space (last accessed March 12, 2025).

Liberation Front. A foundational inspiration for *Bestiario de Lengüitas*, the poem is a litany mourning the accumulation of corpses left by the Argentinian dictatorship (1976–83). The workshop took place during an open-studios weekend. People were coming in and out to sit with us on the floor, on carpets and cushions, or simply to listen and observe what was going on—the shifting collective formations assembling around the translations. Many languages filled our room (I remember hearing Spanish, Japanese, and Czech), while only a handful were shared by more than a few people at a time—Frenches included.

At first, the idea of doing a "dirty translation" felt intimidating, a bit sacrilegious, for it rattled the way most of us have been trained or corrected to write and speak properly, in order to succeed at school and, later, at work. This included memories of scorning and discrimination for those who did not conform to the dominant speech norms. Mercedes explained how the writing of *Bestiario* was rooted in the legacy of Néstor Perlongher's *neobarroso*. According to art historian and *Bestiario* collaborator Elena Lespes Muñoz, "The *neobarroso*—a fusion-manifesto of the *barroco* and the *barro*/mud—represents 'la lepra creadora que corroe los estilos oficiales del bien decir,' 'esa lengua amputada deslizando la baba.' In other words, it's a tongue freed from its mouth, which slobbers, marks and transforms everything it finds in its path."[86] During the

86   Elena Lespes Muñoz, "Lenguas como calcetines, Socks that Stink and Tongues that Stick," trans. Annie-Rose Harrison-Dunn, *La Revue* (CAC Brétigny), 2023, https://www.cacbretigny.com/en/846-lenguas-como-calcetines-socks-that-stink-and-tongues-that-stick.

workshop, Mercedes encouraged us to reclaim devalued forms of expression (provincial accents, regional turns of phrase, *mauvais français* [bad French or any other language], spelling mistakes, slang) that testified to the diversity of our social positions and linguistic baggage, unsmoothed and untamed by the dominant codes of proper, public speech. We remembered the stories of shame and rejection, of joy and belonging attached to our faulty uses of language. And we played them on our tongues, regurgitating them in batches of heterolingual slang.[87]

We became hosts to *cadáveres*, to *meufs* and *mioches*, to *jecizi laprdaju kao carape* and *les langues silenciées*. It was a way of remembering, too, the exiled and the dead inhabiting the poem, without embalming them in a frozen reverence; of keeping them vivid through our words, our writings, our voices. We tried to choose what sounded like the "less right" options, listing possible variations that reflected our respective trajectories through languages, filling up

She quotes here from Perlongher's own words: "The creative leprosy corrodes the official styles of proper speech" (*Prosa Plebeya: Ensayos 1980–1992* [1996; Buenos Aires: Colihue, 2008], 94); "this amputated tongue that spills its drool" ("Moreira," in *Poemas completos (1980–1992)* [Buenos Aires: Seix Barral Biblioteca Breve, 1997], 72. Translated to French by Elena Lespes Muñoz, and to English from the French by Annie-Rose Harrison-Dunn.

[87] "My definition of a 'heterolingual' text is a text staging another tongue as more or less different according to a continuum where the borders are denationalized, denaturalized and graduated." Myriam Suchet, "Heterolinguality as Alternative Imaginary of 'Self': Voices, Democracy and Ethos," *Transversal*, July 2013, https://transversal.at /transversal/0613/suchet/en.

the empty spaces surrounding the original poem with all these other words and voices. Our polyglot bodies bending over the printed texts spread across the floor. Our handwriting overlapping on the sheets of paper. We laughed a lot. And the sound of our tongues populating the air, mixing with the recording of Perlongher's voice playing from Mercedes's computer, formed a dissonant yet generative chorus of transnational-translational bodies.

*

Such collective translation exercises facilitate embodied engagements with language, which open paths for critical movements of decentering via the mutual contamination of positions and perspectives. That said, my own translation activities predominantly take place within the epistemic and discursive framework of two dominant, imperial languages: English and French. In her seminal article "The Politics of Translation," Gayatri Chakravorty Spivak warns of the double bind in which a feminist and decolonial pedagogical translation project is caught in the Anglophone academic context, especially when it involves writings by "women from the Third World" (as she coined): on the one hand, translation is a necessary gesture of feminist solidarity; on the other, it runs the risk of homogenizing a variety of positions and styles, delivering them in a flat "translatese" that eventually fuels an ethnocentrist, imperialist take on these writings. In other words, blindly relying on an imperialist language such as English to stage encounters with transnational, feminist, and anti-imperialist positions is reductive, if

not contradictory. Furthermore, for her, "if you are inter-
ested in talking about the other, and/or in making a claim
to be the other, it is crucial to learn other [nonimperial]
languages."[88]

Spivak's warnings remind us that, even when it is
approached as a mode of unlearning and decentering,
translation always contributes to a kind of knowledge
appropriation and accumulation, especially in academic
contexts. However, there exist various possibilities for
destabilizing—if not escaping—this capitalist enterprise,
which became instrumental in Qalqalah قلقلة's collective
approach to translation. For each text we have commissioned or republished, we discuss the modalities under
which it will, or will not, be translated into the platform's
other languages. Each text thus occasions a discussion
about the context of its production, the modalities of
its circulation, and what would it mean to address it in a
different language.

We also constantly strive to address our respective
relationships to each of the platform's languages, and how
they inform our positions, our interactions, and our collective work. These relationships are indeed enmeshed in
heterogenous postcolonial legacies and marked by divergent racialized and gendered experiences. While the
two white members of our group (including myself) are
native French speakers, other members acquired that language while growing up in countries formerly colonized

88   Gayatri Chakravorty Spivak, "The Politics of Translation"
(1993), in *The Translation Studies Reader*, ed. Lawrence Venuti
(New York: Routledge, 2000), 407.

by France, where the French language continues to serve neocolonial agendas and reinforce class divisions. On another end, Vir Andres Hera, who grew up in Mexico, asserts their choice to work in French as a means of decentering their approach to colonial and decolonial histories and experiences, and of maintaining a transversal, transnational position. Our collective thus never speaks or writes an univocal, neutral French: we work through heterogenous Frenches, marked by colonial legacies, loss, desire, or political struggle. These marks may or may not be apparent but their presence is always acknowledged. When we write or translate collectively into Frenches, we strive to reflect the diversity of these positions into the text, even when they manifest through unruly uses of grammar or vocabulary. In my case, this meant questioning my own sense of entitlement. I vividly remember a time when I set to edit and rectify a text that we had written collectively: one of us called out my homogenizing tendencies and the power dynamic I had established with the rest of the group.

The politics of language and translation are also enacted on a very material level in Qalqalah قلقلة. For example, the fact that our economy rarely allows for fair compensation of professional translators leads to disparities in who is able to provide that labor. Only three members of the collective are proficient enough in written Arabic to translate into that language, which places an additional burden onto these persons. Another outcome of this is the unequal balance of languages on the platform. Despite our efforts, there is less Arabic content than French and English, since all members of the collective are able to work in the latter two languages. However, this observation is not a dead end; it reveals the productive tensions and negotiations that are played out through translation and collective work and are interwoven with economic realities as much as political ones.

*

In her essay "Many Englishes: On Editing and Power," writer Mirene Arsanios reflects on writing and being edited (by her former partner) in nonnative English, and on her own role as an editor for *Makhzin*, a bilingual literary magazine in English and Arabic. She asks:

> How do you (I) edit a text in a language you (I) don't have full command of? When an author asks, "Can I say this?" I must fight my own (internalized) (oppressive) inclinations in trying to get a text as grammatically neutral as possible. What linguistic standards am I applying when editing? Who are these corrections for? [...] When writing, translating and editing, how to not perpetuate the patriarchy of the monolingual nation-state, the colonizer? How to preserve the texture and poetics of a voice translating itself without celebrating the error or failure of the "outsider"—all tropes assigned to the non-Western other, or that we, non-Westerners, sometimes deliberately occupy.[89]

89 Mirene Arsanios, "Many Englishes: On Editing and Power," Mophradat, https://mophradat.org/wp-content/uploads /2021/09/Mirene-Arsanios_Many-Englishes.pdf. It originally appeared in *Vida*, July 30, 2017 (link discontinued).

Such questions are also at the core of both Qalqalah قلقلة's work and my own work as a translatress. When I started, I was sometimes challenged by the diversity of Englishes that I encountered: I realized that I could not use the same approach for a text written with panache and humor by a native speaker with perfectly mastered language play as for one composed by a nonnative person with more or less fluency, or for an English translation from an original text in a third language. In such cases, the labor of translation offers a hands-on engagement with some of the issues addressed by Hito Steyerl in her much-discussed article "International Disco Latin," which echoes Mirene Arsanios's preoccupations.[90]

Steyerl wrote her text in response to "International Art English," an essay by Alix Rule and David Levine, published online the year before. In it, the authors scrutinized "the curious lexical, grammatical, and stylistic features of what [they] call International Art English [...] and speculate on the future of this language through which contemporary art is created, promoted, sold, and understood."[91] For Rule and Levine, IAE "has everything to do with English, but it is emphatically not English." Using a lexical analysis software, they set to parse—in a mocking, at times derogatory tone—the vocabulary and syntax of e-flux Announcements as the paragon of a grandiloquent,

90   Hito Steyerl, "International Disco Latin," *e-flux journal*, no. 45 (May 2013), https://www.e-flux.com/journal/45/60100 /international-disco-latin/.

91   Alix Rule and David Levine, "International Art English," *Triple Canopy*, no. 16 (2012), https://tc3.canopycanopycanopy .com/contents/international_art_english.

yet faulty, use of English language by global international art workers (such as myself). More interestingly to me, the authors trace the genealogy of this jargon back to the pages of *October*, a journal of art criticism founded in 1976, which imported the theories and vocabulary of France's poststructuralists and Germany's Frankfurt School into English via translation and self-translation. According to Rule and Levine, "the progeny of *October* elevated accidents of translation to the level of linguistic norms," contributing to the reproduction of an elitist art world whose agents acknowledge and valorize each other based on the (wobbly) use of IAE.

In her flamboyant response, Steyerl underlines what Rule and Levine's essay fails to address and, in fact, exemplifies: the imperialist distinction that is enforced between, on the one hand, underpaid/unpaid art laborers, precarious students, and nonnative speakers relying on a deviant use of English; and, on the other hand, a native or international elite who can afford an expensive education into correct, sanctioned English. As Steyerl remarks, "IAE is an accurate expression of social and class tensions around language and circulation within today's art worlds and markets: a site of conflict, struggle, contestation, and often invisible and gendered labor." She celebrates and embraces this "digital lingua franca" and its glitches, as it drafts, for her, the promise of a renewed audience unsettling geographical and class boundaries. Overturning the elitist vision of Rule and Levine, she adds that, "after all, IAE is *also* a language of dissidents, migrants, and renegades. [...] So we—the anonymous crowd of people (which includes myself) sustaining and actually living this language—might want to alienate that language even further, make it more foreign, and decisively cut its ties to any imaginary original."

I've always loved this text: in a way, I find it insincere (a language of renegades, really?), but its beauty, humor, and fury are nevertheless galvanizing. Rereading it in recent years, it led me to question my own practice as a (co-)editor and (co-)translatress in English and French—or rather, in "many Englishes," as Arsanios would say, and many Frenches. How could a translation practice reflect, and shelter such deviant uses of language in order to host, and care for heterogenous or marginalized positions that resist the normalizing templates of grammar—without instrumentalizing or exoticizing them in turn? How could the collective transformation of language via acts of writing, editing, translation, or speech become a stage through which to articulate our political claims and divergent subjectivities while forging and witnessing the affective bonds and the disagreements weaving through them?

Translating Blackness
and the Labor of Adjacency

In the fall of 2018, I attended "The Sojourner Project: Dialogues on Black Precarity, Fungibility, and Futurity," organized by the Practicing Refusal Collective, at the Columbia Global Center in Paris.[92] The event intended to

---

92   Formed in 2015 by Tina Campt and Saidiya Hartman,
        the Practicing Refusal Collective is "an international Black

address global and local manifestations of anti-blackness in relation to decolonization and postcoloniality, and possible feminist responses to it. The program specifically asked: "What are [the] national or regional idioms or inflections [of anti-blackness]?" and "How do these critical terms travel or translate?" The discussions took place in English, with live interpretation into French. Toward the very end of the roundtable, one of the speakers spontaneously asked the interpreter how she had been translating "blackness" throughout the discussion. The entire audience turned toward the interpreter, a white woman who had been performing her work unseen from the back of the room for the last two hours. She put aside the microphone that connected her only to the audience's headphones, and answered out loud: "Identité noire." The speaker frowned in surprise. Whispers of uneasiness were heard. Then, a brief silence.

As several speakers had remarked during the conference, the very notion of blackness encompasses diverse realities that are embedded in the specificity of local contexts and discourses—or the absence of it.[93] As a corollary, "blackness" does not translate easily. Like other untranslatable terms, it demands a careful, situated approach, one taking into account its past, current, and future

feminist forum of artists and scholars dedicated to initiating new dialogues on blackness, anti-black violence, and black futurity in the twenty-first century." See The Sojourner Project, https://www.thesojournerproject.org/about/.

93   As Maboula Soumahoro, one of the speakers, pointed out during the conference: "In France, racial categories operate in silence."

circulations, as shown by the increased dissemination of Black US authors across French academic, artistic, and activist networks thanks to translation projects.[94] I often hear French-speaking colleagues and friends using the English word when overtly or implicitly referencing theories of blackness stemming from the United States.

In the French context, "blackness" has been addressed via a diversity of terms. One of its historical precursors is *négritude*, a word forged by writer and politician Aimé Césaire in the 1930s in conversation with other Black intellectuals such as Léopold Sédar Senghor, when France was still a thriving colonial empire. In her article "Négritude et philosophie," Nadia Yala Kisukidi describes this vibrant political and literary movement with ties to the 1920–30s Harlem Renaissance in the United States, which accompanied the rise of Pan-Africanism and anti-colonialism on a global scale.[95] Négritude was later criticized by authors such as Frantz Fanon who, while acknowledging its political and intellectual importance, denounced it as essentializing, freezing blackness into an enclosed set of traditions that eventually reinstated differentiation and racism. Kisukidi recently recalled that "the meaning of the notion of Négritude shifts according to

94   One could cite, for example, the translations of several books by bell hooks, published by Cambourakis and Divergences since 2015; the anthology of translated texts *Black feminism. Anthologie du féminisme africain-américain, 1975–2000*, ed. Elsa Dorlin (Paris: L'Harmattan, 2020); or *Les sous-communs: Planification fugitive et étude noir* (Paris: Brook, 2022), a collective translation of Harney and Moten, *Undercommons*.

95   Nadia Yala Kisikudi, "Négritude et philosophie," *Rue Descartes* 83, no. 4 (2015), 1–15.

history, its locations, its poets."* Nevertheless, or some-times because of that, the term has been claimed by a few contemporary translators as a potential, albeit notori-ously disputable, French translation for blackness.

Maboula Soumahoro, one of the guest speak-ers present at Columbia Paris that afternoon, used the phrase "identité noire" in her book *Le triangle et l'hexagone: Réflexions sur une identité noire*—in which she retraces her own trajectory as a Black scholar between France and the US, addressing her construction as a Black subject amidst French systemic racism, in dialogue with a variety of inter-national thinkers, activists, and artists.[96] In recent years, the term *noirceur* (a literal translation of blackness) has been claimed by several thinkers, including Norman Ajari and Kisukidi. For Ajari, embracing the metaphorics of "the obscure, the sinister, the negative"* that have histor-ically been associated with the term Black and its lexical field is a necessity.[97] Taking a different approach, Kisukidi chooses to detach *noirceur* from a strictly racial dimension to embrace a wider array of minority languages, writings, and practices.[98] The neologisms *noiritude* and *noirité* (a counterpart to *blanchité*—whiteness) also began to cir-culate, moving away from the semantic fields of color and

---

96 The book was published in English as *Black Is the Journey, Africana the Name*, trans. Kaiama Glover (Hoboken, NJ: Wiley, 2022).

97 Norman Ajari, *Noirceur. Race, genre, classe et pessimisme dans la pensée africaine-américaine au XXIᵉ siècle* (Paris: Éditions Divergences, 2022)

98 Nadia Yala Kisukidi, interview, *Ballast*, July 2, 2020, https://www.revue-ballast.fr/nadia-yala-kisukidi-le-conflit-nest-pas-entre-le-particulier-et-luniversel.

obscurity to emphasize sociohistorical processes. These
are just a few examples gathered through readings and
conversations, and a more rigorous inquiry would be
necessary to do justice to the diverse and evolving ways
that individuals and communities articulate blackness
for themselves and for others, either in translation or
directly in French.

What was striking in the conference, is how the term
blackness had been taken for granted by Anglophone
speakers who were all familiar with the specific academic and activist contexts in which the term circulated,
most specifically in the United States. Given its complex,
layered history in translation and in the French-speaking
context, several people in the audience wondered why had
this not been discussed with the interpreter in advance—
especially given that "How do these critical terms travel
or translate?" had been one of the event's guiding questions. As another translator once said to me in a private
conversation: "Interpreters are only noticed when a
problem arises." The sudden exposure of the interpreter
revealed a disconnect between intellectual and theoretical approaches to translation, and the daily working
realities of translators and interpreters—who are often
invisibilized, undervalued, and underpaid. Fortunately,
some audience members promptly reacted, and a great,
unexpected discussion on the racial/colonial politics of
translation unfolded through the room. Françoise Vergès,
one of the guest speakers, asked how to build a transnational subaltern language, a language that one does not
need to know in order to feel close to. For her, translating blackness should go against the Western concept of

transparency, the colonial demand to understand everything. She continued (I quote here from my notes): "Blackness as translation is to say: Yes, I can be foreign, I can be made foreign." Riffing on the idea of blackness as translation, another speaker, Denise Ferreira da Silva, added: "We have to live with the precariousness of translation."

In the audience, writer and film producer Olivier Marboeuf asked on what grounds a translator should be accredited; which background, education, or professional training gives someone the right to translate any text or discourse? Somebody quoted Black US poet John Keene who, in his article "Translating Poetry, Translating Blackness," regrets "the absence of translated black voices" from across the globe; and calls for "not only more translators, but more *black* translators [... to] step into the breach to undertake this work."[99] Maboula Soumahoro concluded that translating blackness should involve trusting people who are not trained, accredited translators; and opening nonofficial, alternative channels of translation. The interpreter did not participate in this discussion. She went on with her mission, in the back of the room.

These discussions regularly came back to my mind, notably in 2022, when I translated a conversation between Soumahoro, US artist Xaviera Simmons, and curator Savannah Wood about Simmons's forthcoming

---

[99] John Keene, "Translating Poetry, Translating Blackness," *Poetry Foundation* (blog), April 28, 2016, https://www.poetryfoundation.org/featured-blogger/74906/translating-poetry-translating-blackness.

exhibition "Nectar" at Kadist.[100] At the time, Soumahoro was working on her French translation of Saidiya Hartman's *Lose Your Mother*.[101] "What I didn't expect was the boldness that it would require," she said. "It was not just an academic exercise, it was about breaking a French silence and voicing certain things in French." She added that one of the main challenges, for her, was to find a suitable translation for blackness. She pointed out that it was not "a matter of inventing, but of finding the strength to impose new terms" in French discourse. These terms would then be opened up to discussion and debate, hopefully leading to intellectual and political transformations. She concluded: "I can't wait for that translation to be challenged. That would mean that the conversation will have started." Her position offered both a humbling and liberatory model, turning untranslatability into an opportunity for public discussion, collective unlearning and empowerment. It also positioned translators—in her case, a self-taught, "unaccredited" translatress—as key agents in that process.

100 Published as "A Conversation Between Xaviera Simmons, Maboula Soumahoro and Savannah Wood," *Xaviera Simmons: Nectar*, exhibition leaflet, Kadist, Paris, 2022, https://kadist.org/wp-content/uploads/2022/04/WRK-KDST-nectar-20221805-digital.pdf.

101 Her translation, *À perte de mère—Sur les routes atlantiques de l'esclavage* was published by Brook in September 2023. Unfortunately, it had not yet been released when I wrote this text.

*

In the spring of 2021, a passionate debate unfolded across international media regarding the translations of Black US poetess Amanda Gorman's "The Hill We Climb," a poem she had performed during US president Joe Biden's inauguration ceremony that January. Several opinion columns appeared in international newspapers, following the decommissioning of Catalan writer and translator Victor Obiols—on the basis, according to him, that "they were looking for a different profile, that of a woman: young, activist—and preferably Black."*[102] Another translator—white, nonbinary writer Marieke Lucas Rijneveld—had resigned after a public controversy around publishing house Meulenhoff's hiring them to translate Gorman's poem into Dutch. That choice was deemed profit-oriented by its critics, as Rijneveld had just received the International Booker Prize. Offended (often white and male) translators fiercely claimed that nobody should tell them what they have the right to translate or not. On the opposite end, several authors preferred to address, as John Keene did, the structural misrecognition of Black creators, writers, and translators by established publishing houses and institutions.

102 AFP, "'Ils cherchaient un profil différent': le traducteur en catalan de la poétesse Amanda Gorman remercié," *Le Monde*, March 11, 2020, https://www.lemonde.fr/culture/article /2021/03/11/ils-cherchaient-un-profil-different-le-traducteur -en-catalan-de-la-poetesse-amanda-gorman-remercie _6072702_3246.html

Ultimately, it was in a text by translatress and curator Canan Marasligil, "Uncaring: Reflections on the Politics of Literary Translation," that I found the most balanced and insightful analysis.[103] Speaking from her position as the daughter of Turkish Muslim immigrants in Western Europe, which informs her practice as a translatress as well as her acknowledgment by the publishing industry, Marasligil deplored how the debate was framed by sensationalist calls for political correctness and cancel culture, thus misreading more significant contextual issues. The problem, she argued, was "one of representation, as well as accessibility, and therefore: power. Who gets to tell which stories and how, matters, as well as who translates them for whom, and in which context." She explained:

> To be clear, most of the criticism [...] did not say that literary translators need to have the exact same identities and experiences as the author, and therefore that no white person can ever translate a black author. They rightfully challenged the publisher's choice in a context of ongoing systemic racism against non-white Dutch voices, and especially black ones. [...] Amanda Gorman's poetry falls into the category where the political context matters greatly, and the translation of her poetry is a possibility to break through the "frozen state" of many identities, elevated and silenced at the comfort and benefit of the dominant gatekeepers.

103 Canan Marasligil, "Uncaring: Reflections on the Politics of Literary Translation," *The Attention Span* (newsletter), March 4, 2021, https://cananmarasligil.net/read/uncaring -reflections-on-the-politics-of-literary-translation.

> As we breathe new languages into her experience
> and imagination, we should care to create space for
> inclusion and recognition.

I found this debate enlightening for various reasons:
first of all, it updated and popularized discussions on
translation theory, translation politics, and the publishing industry that usually remain circumscribed to a
limited circle of specialists. Moreover, as several authors
remarked, it took place only a few months after the Black
Lives Matter movement spread worldwide following the
murder of George Floyd by Minneapolis police officers
on May 26, 2020. At the time, many international artistic and cultural institutions engaged in public discussions
about possible courses of action within their means to
fight against anti-blackness, racism, and police violence.
Art workers and audiences demanded structural changes
to foster inclusion and representation within these very
institutions, starting with their staff and modes of organization. The way established publishing houses missed the
opportunity to actualize these demands when commissioning translations for Gorman's poem, was thus more
acutely perceived as a sign of disregard. In the French
context—where publisher Fayard was praised for hiring
Congolese Belgian musician and singer Lous and the
Yakuza for the translation of Gorman's poem—the debate
was framed in relation to the so-called republican critique of "communitarianism," "separatism," and "cancel
culture." The political role of translation—as a mode of
knowledge production, as a social practice, and as a gendered and racialized form of labor—was thus publicly

instantiated and addressed, crystallizing urgent political and societal issues.

These debates reverberated into recurrent discussions that I had with fellow translators, especially white, feminist, self-taught translatresses like myself. Were we being complicit in unbalanced power structures and processes of silencing when we earned money translating texts addressing blackness or other vulnerable experiences—while Black and racialized scholars and activists also denounced the recuperation of their struggles, labor, and voices by academic and artistic institutions who may only perform "surface-level antiracism"?[104] Could translation nevertheless become a way of enacting gestures of solidarity, support, and allyship by contributing to the dissemination of voices and bodies affected by, and fighting against, systemic racism? These questions should be asked again and again, among ourselves, with affected people and communities, and to commissioning institutions. They may also be posed differently when these translations are paid, individual jobs; and when they are collective, volunteer endeavors, motivated by the

---

104 Geneva-based anti-racist and feminist scholar, activist, and cultural worker Noémi Michel explains how, after the global spread of the Black Lives Matter movement, she suddenly faced numerous requests from the media and academic institutions who sought to exploit her work and her experience without implementing structural changes, and without acknowledging her grief and exhaustion. See Michel, "'Do You Consent to Our Care?': From Racial Burden to Black Feminist Dreams," in *Tout ce qu'on tait on sait / We Know What Remains Unsaid*, vol. 2, ed. Wages for Wages Against (Brussels: L'Amazone; Geneva: Privilege, 2023).

desire to engage with a specific text and context, as I will discuss later.

*

In the late summer of 2020, a private art foundation asked me to translate an essay by Black US artist and activist Dread Scott, "America God Damn," originally published in the *Art Newspaper* as a reaction to the murder of George Floyd and the ensuing protests.[105] Active in both the United States and France, the foundation offered to pay for the French translation and the re-publication of the original essay in the free, independent magazine *Zérodeux* in order to participate in the dissemination in France of Black-led US discourse on anti-blackness. First, I hesitated to accept, suggesting that they could find someone whose position would be closer to that of the author. But they convinced me to take the job, with an argument similar to that expressed by translator Samuel Vriezen: "Translating is not about knowing whether we know the experience of the other, it is about being able to acknowledge that this experience is other."[106]

105 Dread Scott, "America God Damn," *Art Newspaper*, June 5, 2020, https://www.theartnewspaper.com/2020/06/05/dread-scott-america-god-damn.

106 Catherine De Kock and Peter Jacobs, "Le poème d'Amanda Gorman doit-il absolument être traduit par une femme noire?," trans. Fabrice Claes, *Daar Daar*, March 2, 2021, https://daardaar.be/rubriques/opinions/le-poeme-damanda-gorman-doit-il-absolument-etre-traduit-par-une-femme-noire/.

I thus approached this translation with a double sense of responsibility: toward the text itself, and toward the experiences it conveyed. This turned out to be one of the most challenging works of translation that I had to undertake individually so far. Dread Scott's text was fiery, lyrical—structured around a litany of "What has changed?" repeated nine times. It was literally inflamed—fueling concrete and metaphorical eruptions of fire, starting with: "The people have learned to write with fire and it is a language understood around the world. Smoldering police stations. Flaming police cars. Blazing barricades. Smoke billowing around the White House." It was a combat text, written by an experienced activist, underlining that there is "no hope without rage."[107]

Dread Scott describes the police murders of Ahmaud Arbery, Breonna Taylor, George Floyd, and Michael Brown. He often uses the word "lynched," meaning killed without trial. The verb immediately brings to mind the black-and-white photographs of murdered Black bodies surrounded by merry white crowds. It signaled the historical continuity of anti-Black violence leading to the deaths of Ahmaud Arbery, Breonna Taylor, George Floyd, and Michael Brown. Their names were already familiar to me, but at the time I was not aware of all their stories. Looking for accurate translations, my throat dried and my fingers

107 This is a quote from Paul Chan's poem "The New No's," presented alongside Dread Scott's work in the group exhibition "An Incomplete History of Protest," Whitney Museum of American Art, New York, August 2017–August 2018. Scott discusses the poem in a 2018 video published by the museum: https://whitney.org/whitney-stories/dread-scott.

trembled, as I was reading news articles and media state-
ments, and writing: *pourchassé*, *sommairement abattu*, *cesser
de respirer*, *tuée*, *tué*, *tueurs*, *meurtriers*. I understood the
necessity of naming, precisely, the circumstances of these
persons' assassinations, in French. To truly acknowledge
the shattering violence and injustice of their death. To
fuel the rage Dread Scott was writing about—the rage to
change. I discerned more clearly how translation could
contribute to igniting or sustaining that rage, by engaging
closely with the violence reflected in these words, and by
disseminating it across languages.

   Through this process, I kept thinking of the way
Black feminist scholar Tina Campt describes the "labor of
adjacency."[108] In an initial, concise statement, she defines
it as "the reparative work of transforming proximity into
accountability; the labor of positioning oneself in relation to another in ways that revalue and redress complex
histories of dispossession." Her forging of the concept
of adjacency stems from her encounter with the moving-
image work of Luke Willis Thompson, a New Zealander
artist of Fijian heritage. Thompson produced a series of
black and white, silent filmic portraits of Black individuals who lost loved ones to police violence.[109] *Autoportrait*

---

108   Tina Campt, "Black Visuality and the Practice of Refusal,"
        Women & Performance 29, no. 1 (2019), https://www
        .womenandperformance.org/ampersand/29-1/campt.

109   They are Diamond Reynolds, whose partner Philando Castile
        was murdered next to her and her daughter in their car
        in Falcon Heights, Minnesota, in 2016; Brandon, grandson
        of Dorothy Groce, who was shot by police in her home in
        Brixton, London, in 1985; and Graeme, son of Joy Gardner,
        killed by police in her home in Crouch End, London, in 1993.

(2017), which features a silent Diamond Reynolds, prompted critiques accusing the artist of exploiting and aestheticizing Black pain. In her careful analysis, Campt describes it instead as "a practice of quiet witnessing" and "an act of refusal":

> It is a refusal to be complicit in the silencing of black pain and suffering; and a simultaneous refusal to impose words on the indescribable. It is a refusal to depoliticize the space of the gallery or to assume that the art world is removed from the politics of black fungibility. It is a refusal that forces us to do the work of adjacency by reckoning both inside the gallery and beyond it with our own relationship, our own positioning within the infrastructures of anti-black violence that pervade every space, regardless of whether we acknowledge it or not.

Although the kind of proximity that Campt refers to in her initial definition arises from a shared association with blackness, she later broadens the scope of positions from which one could engage in the "affective labor of adjacency." According to her, that labor "requires us to feel beyond the security of our own situation and cultivate instead an ability to confront the precarity of less valued or actively devalued individuals, and doing the ongoing work of sustaining a relationship to these imperiled and precarious bodies." She adds—and I find her use of the pronoun "you" very powerful, for it calls the reader (me, you, us) out—that such work does not "allow you to put yourself in the place of another, nor does it allow you to presume you share the pain or suffering of differently racialized subjects. It is recognizing a disparity between your respective situations and working to address it [...] and choosing to feel across that difference rather than with or for someone in very different circumstances."

Campt's proposal is inscribed in the realm of vision, where she complexifies the relationship between subjects who engage in various, reciprocal acts of looking. However, I believe that the kind of labor she describes and calls for could be transposed to the realm of text, and embodied in a practice of translation. Engaging with her reflections while translating Dread Scott's text was both helpful and challenging: it called on me to reconsider my position as a translatress, not as a mere conveyor of words, but as a witness. A witness both to what was described in the text—"sustaining a relationship to [...] imperiled and precarious bodies"; and to what was actually happening beyond the textual realm, out in the world—namely systemic racism, anti-Black violence, death, loss, and pain, as well as revolts, and commitments to end that violence and that pain. The ethical question that must then be asked is: How to turn witnessing from a passive act to an active engagement? In that particular case, translation offered a way to testify to the violence as well as the revolts: to name and describe them in a different language, and attest to their existence in that language—i.e., in French, a language in which systemic racism is too often denied by those in power. Through translation, the act of witnessing—and the labor of adjacency—become a shared responsibility, jointly carried by translatresses, commissioners, publishers, and readers. That experience also pushed me to make my translation practice more collective, in order to confront a diversity of situated positions, interpretations, and relationships to words, and to the stories and experiences that they convey.

The Messy "We" of Collective Translation

In late spring 2020, during the first Covid-19 lockdown in France, a dozen members of a French feminist group of art workers convened for an online discussion. Prior to the pandemic, our group used to meet every month in public spaces to discuss ways of undoing the sexist, racist, and toxic neoliberal logics pervading the arts ecosystem in France. Our discussions often took on an intimate tone, sharing personal testimonies and experiences. The group also undertook actions to support victims of abuse, harassment, or discrimination in their professional contexts. On that evening, we met online for the first time, watching our tired, worried faces distributed across the grid of our screens. I remember our gloomy voices expressing fear, exasperation, and feelings of powerlessness—and our craving for physical reunions and collective action.

At the time, I was still recovering from my first bout of Covid, which left me exhausted, voiceless, and breathless for several weeks. While listening, I looked at the lush forest out the window, conscious that unlike my interlocutors, I was incredibly lucky to have moved to a rural area just before the pandemic broke out. From the start, our house was meant to be open to friends and art workers. But under the circumstances, its potential as a hospitable working and living space had to stay dormant for a while.

My failing body reactivated the memory of gradually falling sick while battling against damaging working conditions in my last institutional job. My family and I moved out of Paris after I left my job and lost my salary. In a way, it was institutional sickness that had brought me here—to this house, and to translation. Two years later, I was able to see how, out of those feelings of loss, isolation, and failure, powerful things had blossomed. Because when I was finally able to articulate a complaint, it was heard, bringing me into an alliance of women with whom I found (and was later able to return) trust, care, and reparation. They were the very same persons who were now looking at me from across the screen, feeling blocked and separated.

On that night, we spoke again about the impact that Sara Ahmed's work had on many of us. Back then, none of her books and only a handful of articles had been translated into French—although she offered precious tools and tactics that seemed so adequate to the growing struggles against discrimination and abuse in French art institutions and schools.[110] We felt a double urgency:

---

110 As far as we knew, only two French translations of Ahmed's writing were available at the time: "Les rabat-joie féministes (et autres sujets obstinés)," trans. Oristelle Bonis, *Cahiers du Genre* 53, no. 2 (2012); and "Le language de la diversité," trans. Noémie Grunenwald, *GLAD!*, no. 7 (2019). Since then, other translations have been published, including *Vandalisme queer*, trans. Emma Bigé (Romainville: Burn-Août, 2020); "Orientations. Vers une phénoménologique queer," trans. Emma Bigé and Daphné Pons *Multitudes*, no. 82 (2021); "Les murs de l'université," trans. Aurore Turbiau, *Fabula-LhT*, no. 26 (2021), https://www.fabula.org/lht/26/ahmed.html; and "Plainte et survie," by a collective of ENSAPC students, *Show* (2021).

gathering around her texts, to hang out with her words and with each other; as well as disseminating her thoughts in the French context to readers who may otherwise be discouraged by the complexity of her writing in English. Primarily though, we wanted an occasion to reunite, a hope that we would be able to spend time together again. Translation offered itself as a pretext for deep encounters and as "a location for healing,"[111] as a home and a refuge. A place from which to depart again, branch out, spread, leak—like Ahmed's complainers and killjoys leaving messy and unwanted traces across institutional corridors, hijacking space, claiming presence. Hence, a temporary translation collective assembled—with Emilie Renard, Victorine Grataloup, Julie Pellegrin, Rosanna Puyol, Barbara Sirieix, and myself. The story that follows could be told in many different ways; this is only one possible, subjective account of our work together.

*

We first met at my house in August 2020. Sara Ahmed's writings accompanied us in the garden, in the forest, or in the kitchen while we reconnected with the exhilarating feeling of being together, breathing, reading, and

---

111 "I saw in theory then a location for healing. [...] I found a place where I could imagine possible futures, a place where life could be lived differently. [...] When our lived experience of theorizing is fundamentally linked to processes of self-recovery, of collective liberation, no gap exists between theory and practice." bell hooks, "Theory as Liberatory Practice," in *Teaching to Transgress: Education as the Practice of Freedom* (London: Routledge, 1994).

cooking together with the vegetables we harvested from the garden. After discussing several texts, we chose to translate "Feminists at Work: Complaint, Diversity, Institutions."[112] In this text, written for a 2019 conference and published on her blog, Ahmed explains how her participation in a series of inquiries into sexual harassment and sexual misconduct led her to study complaints, interviewing students, academics, and administrators about their experience of the complaint process in academia. The testimonies she recounts and her analysis of the university as a "complaint graveyard" can appear discouraging, if not infuriating at first. Yet one story seems to turn the tables: a PhD student, forced to leave the campus after lodging a complaint about a powerful professor, was approached by other students who wanted to learn from her experience. The student called it "an unexpected little gift." She realized that, although her complaint appeared to have failed and backfired, she acquired knowledge that she was now able to share with others: her experience became a resource for collective struggle. "A complaint is a way of communicating with others. It forms a transgenerational collective," Ahmed said during a talk at EHESS in Paris in June 2019. This realization, that the shattering, individual experience of complaining could be turned into collective knowledge and agency, was a precious, reparative gift. We wanted to translate that gift for others; and

---

112 Sara Ahmed, "Feminists at Work," *Feminist Killjoys* (blog), January 10, 2020, https://feministkilljoys.com/2020/01/10 /feminists-at-work/.

make it available by finding a platform to distribute our translation online and for free.[113]

Over three days, we labored through the text. We first read it together aloud, paragraph after paragraph, with the variety of our accents, intonations, and levels of English fluency. Sometimes our voices trembled with emotion or anger. We paused when a sentence or an expression resisted our understanding or raised a translation problem—there were many! The virtuosity and playfulness of Ahmed's writing make it as hard to read and translate as it is profoundly moving and affective. Textual repetitions often echo, almost hypnotically, the sense of exhaustion and frustration arising from the labyrinth of complaint procedures. We had to twist our language to find ways of writing that would channel these feelings and render Ahmed's sense of rhythm, rather than strictly stick to her words. The arresting quality of her writing also relies on her ability to make the reader stop, rewind, and ask themselves: Did I really read that? What does it mean?

Our desire to leak the text into French grew in parallel with the realization of the difficulty of our task on both linguistic and ethical levels. Although our group was far from being homogenous, it did not include any Black, Indigenous, or People of Color—which is how Ahmed and some of the protagonists in her text introduce themselves, and informs their experience of structural racism and

113 Our translation was published by the fabulous feminist magazine *Panthère Première*, both in print and online, as "Féministes au travail. Travail de diversité, travail de plainte, institution," *Panthère Première*, no. 8 (Fall 2022), https://pantherepremiere.org/texte/feministes-au-travail/.

complaint procedures in academia. We asked ourselves: Considering that we are translating a text addressing diversity through the words of racialized scholars and students, among others, wasn't the composition of our group problematic? However, if we would specifically invite racialized persons to join us in a second phase, after we had already formed a kind of shared intimacy around the text, didn't we run the risk of tokenizing these persons, and leaning on their experiences and knowledge? Although we did not necessarily reach a consensus on these questions, we decided to keep doing the work—trusting our initial shared desire to engage with that specific text. We committed to research and acknowledge the works of other authors and translators who had written about similar issues in French, discussing and learning from their linguistic and ethical choices. Among the texts we read while translating was Fred Moten and Stefano Harney's *The Undercommons*—which was then being collectively translated into French on the initiative of Brook, Rosanna's publishing house. As Julie wrote in the margins of our translation-in-progress: "I find Moten enlightening here: situating our privileged position—ok; but acknowledging that structures of domination, if they are violent for some of us, are consequently violent for all of us—and that if you work toward doing better you have to do it for the other but for yourself as well."*[114]

114 Julie added the following quote: "The coalition emerges out of your recognition that it's fucked up for you, in the same way that we've already recognized that it's fucked up for us. I don't need your help. I just need you to recognize that this shit is killing you, too, however much more softly,

*

We needed two years to complete the translation. Most of our encounters around Ahmed's text (each introduced by a good hour of gossiping) were moments of energizing joy. Yet that long companionship in translation also generated some of the tensions that inevitably accompany collective work—around the division of labor, and around questions of authority, situatedness, and representation. Most of these tensions crystallized toward the end of the process, when we faced the concrete demands of the publisher, feminist magazine *Panthère Première*: setting up deadlines, responding to editorial comments and requests, standardizing "inclusive" writing (against our initial will), reviewing translation choices, and making corrections. This required an enormous amount of time and energy, which some of us no longer had for various professional and personal reasons. At the same time, it displaced the question of responsibility, or rather it brought it back to the forefront: If only half the initial group was able to perform these tasks, up to what point should we seek consensus on the final editorial and translating decisions?

That question crystallized around the writing of a short text, which was intended to introduce the reasons why we wanted to translate Ahmed's essay in the first place, to situate ourselves in relation to it, and to expose our working process and decisions. Based on notes taken during our sessions, three of us—Julie, Barbara, and

you stupid motherfucker, you know?" (Harney and Moten, *Undercommons*, 140–41). I share this with her permission.

myself—set out to write that introduction, which we offered to sign collectively. However, another member of our group, Rosanna, expressed her disagreement.[115] She explained that she did not recognize herself in the generic phrasing that we had initially used to situate our group and did not want the introduction to be signed collectively, as unlike the translation, it did not reflect the diversity of our voices, positions, and desires.

Her comments confronted us with the need to address things that had been left unsaid, or that had wrongly been taken for granted. For example, the way the introduction was written could indeed seem authoritarian: usurping a collective voice, speaking in place of the group rather than on behalf of it, and amalgamating the diversity of our positions toward the text into an artificial, reductive "we." We thus agreed that the three of us who had drafted the initial introduction would rewrite it in a way that would make our "we" less univocal, underlying our plural relationships to, and engagement with, Ahmed's writings and ideas, and that it would be signed by our three names. In light of the discussions, our trio also decided to rewrite the footnotes: instead of a distant, seemingly objective way of delivering contextual and theoretical information to the readers, we opted for situated accounts of our respective encounters with specific concepts and references.

This experience reaffirmed the necessity of constantly articulating the "we" of collective translation; not as an over-encompassing, consensual "we" but, on the

---

115 Our exchanges are recounted here with Rosanna's permission.

contrary, as an agonistic "we," to reflect and complexify the situatedness and interdependence of every translational act. An unresolved "we" that should manifest in the translated text and its paratext; an untranslatable "we" that should be ceaselessly addressed by its constituents throughout the entire working process—for individual positions also evolve over such long durations and differ according to the dynamics of the various groups and situations we find ourselves part of. Through this experience, I learned that identifying and discussing the way power, authority, and privilege are distributed and felt within a group is vital to any kind of collective labor, be it translation-related or otherwise. Especially when affective relations are involved, which is often the case in my own experience. This is also what allows translation to become a space for collective joy—an exhilarating feeling that holds the power to spark, nurture, and sustain different collective struggles.[116]

116　"Joy rarely feels comfortable or easy, because it transforms and reorients people and relationships. Rather than the desire to exploit, control, and direct others, it is resonant with emergent and collective capacities to do things, make things, undo painful habits, and nurture enabling ways of being together." carla bergman and Nick Montgomery, *Joyful Militancy: Building Thriving Resistance in Toxic Times* (Chico, CA: AK Press, 2017), https://theanarchistlibrary.org/library/joyful-militancy-bergman-montgomery.

Staging Translational Encounters
in Performative and Pedagogical Spaces

From 2019 onward, occasions arose to publicly experiment with ways of doing and un/learning with translation, via workshops and seminars that I organized, or co-organized in art schools, choreographic centers, and other cultural institutions. These invitations created a stage through which to openly share some of the aforementioned questions while posing new ones: How to work around the position of authority that is associated with the roles of teaching, organizing, and moderating? How to facilitate embodied modes of collective un/learning via translation? How to make anyone feel invited to engage with translation as a critical and generative practice—regardless of their expertise in language(s) or theory? How to use these situations to materialize a set of tools that could outlive a temporary event and have a lasting, transformative potential for those involved? For bell hooks, teaching implies performativity, reciprocity, and mutual engagement, and relies on "strategies [that] must constantly be changed, invented, reconceptualized."[117] Such a model extends to the kind of translation practice that I tried to introduce during these workshops, which evolved through encounters with different participants, positions, and experiences. To acknowledge them, I often sought to detach translation from a strictly textual practice, experimenting with various ways of engaging the bodies, voices, and accents present.

117 hooks, *Teaching to Transgress, 10–11*.

Often, these workshops and seminars began with, or were structured around, a reflection on language and violence. International participants had to rely on various degrees of proximity to and fluency in a dominant, colonial language (i.e., English or French) as an unequally shared ground for communication. We thus sought to address the disparities, gaps, and hierarchies that our heterogenous relationships to these languages both generated and reflected. We encouraged the presence of other languages (such as Nouchi or Breton), accepting that not everything should be comprehensible by everyone at every moment. In doing so, we shifted the focus from communication to address, thus debunking the dominant role of language as a seemingly transparent vector and container of knowledge, and opening up space for gestures of refusal to emerge as well.[118] In the last part of this essay, I will briefly describe a few practical exercises that I devised for some of these workshops, how they were structured and why, and what they provoked. In doing so, I hope to draft a resource for other educators, students, or art workers who wish to activate the transformative potentials of translation in artistic and academic contexts, and nurture a conversation about them.

---

118 I am indebted to Eve Tuck and K. Wayne Yang's reflections on refusal in "R-Words: Refusing Research," in *Humanizing Research: Decolonizing Qualitative Inquiry with Youth and Communities*, ed. Django Paris and Maisha T. Winn (Los Angeles: Sage, 2014), 223–48.

*

During a public workshop at Tanzquartier Wien in December 2019, I invited participants—mostly local and international choreographers, dancers, and artists—to play with the following quote by Jacques Derrida: "Je n'ai qu'une langue, ce n'est pas la mienne" (I only have one language; it is not mine).[119] In *Monolingualism of the Other*, Derrida evoked the "disorder of identity [*trouble d'identité*]" connected with the traumatic memory of Algerian Jews losing their French citizenship under the Vichy regime.[120] For Derrida, who was ten years old in 1940, this manifested in his exclusion from the French school and thereby from French language. "I do not doubt," he wrote, "that such 'exclusions' come to leave their mark upon this belonging or non-belonging of language, this affiliation to language, this assignation to what is peacefully called a language." Later in the book, Derrida explained that he was never allowed to learn the other languages in use in Algeria—i.e., literary or dialectal Arabic and what were then called Berber languages. The paradoxical statement "I only have one language; it is not mine" is thus anchored in this experience of alienation and debasement that will forever prevent him from considering French language

119   The workshop was organized as part of the series "E N C H A N T É E S, a collection of studies (of joy and) of imagination," convened by choreographer Alix Eynaudi.

120   Jacques Derrida, *Monolingualism of the Other; or, The Prosthesis of Origin*, trans. Patrick Mensah (Stanford, CA: Stanford University Press, 1998), 14. The following quotes appear on 16–17.

as a "home." Derrida's reflections on the relationships of domination, exclusion, and belonging reflected in the languages we speak, lack, or learn may very well resonate beyond French language and the specific colonial experience he recounted. Could the collective dissection, reshuffling, (mis)translation, and (mis)pronunciation of that sentence by different persons, in several languages, trouble our respective apprehensions of these languages in generative ways? Could it elicit mutual listening and attunement to the various positions present?

First, I distributed a collection of English words written on separate sheets of paper that offered an array of possible translations for Derrida's original French sentence. In small groups, participants (most of whom did not speak French and were not native English speakers) had to recompose a plausible English sentence, working together through the linguistic, affective, and political implications of Derrida's proposal. In the process, they had to negotiate with the possibility of translating without necessarily knowing a given language, relying on the groups' diverse knowledge. Following many discussions and negotiations, the three groups read their English sentences to each other: all were different, thus prompting another discussion on the precariousness of translation. After that, I proposed another approach to the sentence through a meditation of sorts, inspired by the dance studio setting. Participants were invited to find a comfortable spot, sitting on cushions or laying down on yoga mats, surrounded by black velvet curtains. Would you like to try?

You can close your eyes if you want to.
Now, untranslate the sentence in a language that
you cultivate, or that cultivates you.
It could be a language that you inhabit, or that
inhabits you.
A language that you feel close to, or very foreign to.
A language that you have acquired or lost.
It could be a mother tongue, a grandmother
tongue, a sister tongue, a national, regional,
or minor tongue.
A language that you cannot remember or that
you cannot learn.
A language that you desire. A language that
you work with.
A language that irritates you.
Or the one that you love with.
Relax your body and your mind.
Let that sentence flow across your body,
through your breathing,
through your heartbeats,
through your veins and your stomach.
Imagine the words traveling through all the parts
of your body,
up until your fingers and down to your toes.
Try to contain it, to let it fill you.

After ten minutes, I invited participants to join the person
closest to them and address their sentence to them in
the language they had chosen. The listener, who did not
necessarily speak or understand that language, would
transcribe it on a sheet of paper, and vice versa. Then, each

person read aloud the sentence they had transcribed to the rest of the group. At the end of the workshop, artists Ruthie Jenrbekova and Maria Vilkovisky, who collaborate under the name of krëlex zentr (creolic center), arranged the multilingual sentences into a score for an impromptu choir, inviting us to sing our translations in different voices and tones, vibrating and laughing together. Their proposal emphasized the role of translation as a gesture of reaching out, anchored in multiple bodies. Whether a message is successfully delivered or not does not matter as much as the mutually transformative relationship established through this act;[121] and as the possibility of commoning across the differences that manifest (partially) in our uses of languages.

*

In January 2023, I was asked to organize a daylong translation workshop for my PhD in Practice comrades at the Academy of Fine Arts in Vienna. There, English is the vehicle for a broad diversity of experiences and research that are often conducted in other languages—some of which have been endangered or affected by English and imperial histories. During our seminars, participants evoked the discrepancy between the tongues in which their research took shape, often in conversation with

---

121 This idea owes a lot to Myriam Suchet's *L'imaginaire hétérolingue. Ce que nous apprennent les textes à la croisée des langues* (Paris: Classiques Garnier, 2014). Of course, it is different when acts of translation have concrete effects on people's futures—in asylum interviews, for example.

family members, activists, or communities from diverse contexts, and the language through which it had to be mediated and reformulated: English. This also raised questions about address: Who do we write for? Our closest interlocutors and companions, or an abstract academic reader? Although these questions exceed language itself, the affective and political registers of the languages we work with constantly permeated our exchanges.

I began the workshop by asking everyone to introduce themselves and their research "in a language other than English." For some, who were used to pitching their research topic in English in this academic context, switching to a different language was uneasy, as if English was stuck to our tongues, refusing to let go. For others, available languages—such as Russian or Spanish—were also associated with past or present histories of violence and domination, which provoked other forms of resistance or struggle. One participant had been learning an endangered Indigenous tongue that used to be spoken in her family, and she explained that she did not know enough of that language to introduce her research in it. That recognition opened up a crack, as my request had unwillingly exposed the loss she was coping with by attempting to learn that language. During this round of introductions, we thus listened both to the sonority of languages that were more or less familiar or foreign to each of us, and to the various degrees of intimacy, emotion, and friction transpiring through the rhythm and volume of our voices.

Then I invited participants to read selected excerpts from a fiction essay by Mirene Arsanios, *Notes on Mother Tongues: Colonialism, Class, and Giving What You Don't*

Have.[122] The text is written from the perspective of "my language," which personifies the author although she claims not to have (only) one: "My language speaks many languages—French, Italian, Arabic, Spanish, and English—none of which she can call home." It is one of the few texts that I have read and reread multiple times over the last years. I find it both illuminating and troubling, with regard to language politics and to more intimate questionings about motherhood and family transmission (or lack thereof). It also reasserts the political dimension of languages, and the complex legacies of power and care that weave through them: "My language believes that you cannot be a language before your acknowledge the genealogies of care and abuse that have produced you as a language," Mirene writes. I hoped that this text could open generative paths for my comrades to tackle their own relationships to languages within the academic framework and beyond, as it had for me.

I invited everyone to choose a sentence from the essay, and work on it through a series of short exercises. I reproduce them below as a way of sharing one possible method of critically approaching the political and affective stakes of language, while experimenting with modalities of writing with, and through, gestures of translation:

122 Mirene Arsanios, *Notes on Mother Tongues: Colonialism, Class and Giving What You Don't Have* (New York: Ugly Duckling Presse, 2020).

1) Translate the sentence into a tongue of your choice: a mother tongue? A father tongue? A lover tongue? A research tongue? A tongue that you cultivate and that cultivates you? Another tongue?

2) Are there words or fragments that don't translate easily in the tongue you chose? For what reasons? Grammatical? Linguistic? Political? Affective? How would you signal this in your translation?

3) Are there things you disagree with or that irritate you in the original sentence? How could your translation argue with the original text?

4) Make room for (a) ghost(s) in your translation.

5) Now, think about rhythm. Translate that sentence again.

6) Remember these successive translations. Now, translate the sentence back into English*es*.

We read these last sentences aloud and listened to each other: one after the other, our voices assembled a poem of sorts, irrigated by our tongues and accents, our feelings, the ghosts, and the rhythms we had introduced to our translations earlier. All these lingered into the air while we listened with intensity and care, in the renewed intimacy of our group.

*

For this particular workshop, I felt it was important not to frame the discussion only from my position as a white European person whose language played a part in the erasure of and discrimination against others. I thus asked another colleague, Serena Lee, to conceive and moderate the second part of the workshop. Serena has been a precious, regular interlocutor during my PhD and beyond, contributing to several Qalqalah قلقلة projects, and her own research and writing processes are infused with a careful attention to languages and epistemologies, and the way they shape our relationships to knowledge and others. Serena invited us to trace the shape of the Chinese word 時 (time) while chatting about language learning, writing systems, and the moral projects sustaining them. These topics elicited, in turn, stories of childhood memories, family transmission, loss, longing, and persistence. Our hands drew clumsily, in directions that our muscles were not trained to follow, while we enjoyed the sensual contact of the brush on paper. Black ink tainted our fingers. Unexpected shapes emerged, while our conversations took serendipitous turns and we were able to let go of some of the tensions generated by the previous part of the workshop, which had stirred, for some, difficult memories and negative feelings.

This brought to my mind another series of workshops, which Serena had organized in London for her project *Second Tongues* in 2019, and which she had described to me while we were installing a version of that work for the exhibition "Qalqalah قلقلة: plus d'une langue" at CRAC Occitanie in 2020. *Second Tongues* departed from the fictional scenario that "in the future, we all speak a second language not of our choosing. It is assigned at birth and selected at random from the history of language, to be learnt and used alongside the mother tongue." This proposal generated a series of questions, ranging from

"Would the notion of family and community change based on the second languages?" to "Would new forms of power emerge, based on new forms of value?" or (one of my favorites) "How much would all of this cost?"[123] Serena invited different groups of people—domestic workers whom she had met through English language classes, linguists, artists—to discuss these questions *while doing something else,* i.e., cooking, drawing, or modeling letters and familiar objects with colorful salt dough. She said that conversations flowed more easily, or differently, when the hands and the body were actively engaged in physical activities. I loved that approach to embodied intelligence, that way of caring for the bodies present and of eliciting speech in convivial, informal ways. Since then, I have regularly returned to *Second Tongues* as a source of inspiration and reflection.

In May 2023, I asked Serena's permission to reactivate *Second Tongues* in a series of workshop that I organized at Le SHED, an art center in Normandy, where I currently live. These workshops, titled "Traduire avec les pieds" (Translating with our feet) were occasions to play with translation in various ways and with/for diverse audiences—with no expertise in translation or foreign languages required—on the contrary. For me, they were occasions to pursue the reflections initiated over the past years with participants who were not necessarily from the cultural or academic field, and to ask whether translation

---

123 All the questions are listed on this incredible website: https://serenalee.hotglue.me/secondtongues (last accessed March 12, 2025).

could offer a hospitable place for social encounters and interactions. Playfulness and adaptability were thus an important part of these workshops.

One session was co-organized with a local social center supporting women who had recently arrived in France. We discussed and orally attempted to translate idiomatic expressions involving body parts in various languages (i.e., "avoir le cœur sur la main" [to be generous], "avoir les yeux plus gros que le ventre" [to be greedy]), which I had collected from friends and drawn on small paper cards. It provoked many laughs and some ferocious comments about gender bias in language. For the session drawing on *Second Tongues*, I devised another series of translation exercises based on Serena's questions, in the form of an exquisite corpse. After each exercise, participants would transmit their responses to the person sitting next to them. Our translation experiments unfolded and responded to each other, like small gifts—funny, clumsy, and tender: a posthumous text message sent by Voltaire to Frederick the Great in SMS slang, a paper fish, a recorded voicemail in an invented language spoken by a mother and son, a song, a folded poem, and even a frog's croak.

Catching Our Breath

With this collection of experiences, I have attempted to draft possible answers to the questions that have guided my work over the past few years: What does translation do? And what can we do with translation? Rather than considering translation an end in itself, or a means of adding new components to the wealth of knowledge encompassed in books, websites, or schools in a variety of languages, I have tried to approach it as a possible method, as a pretext to generate situations of learning and unlearning with others, and as an occasion for other gestures and practices to emerge.

In her book *Unlearning Imperialism*, Ariella Aïsha Azoulay explains that "unlearning imperialism involves different types of '*de-*,' such as decompressing and decoding; '*re-*,' such as reversing and rewinding; and '*un-*' such as unlearning and undoing."[124] Such gestures could be synonymous with and constituent to a method of *un*translating, as they point to a kind of ongoing critical engagement with knowledge, words, and actions. Azoulay designates these gestures as "rehearsals," an activity that she describes as "a mode of being with others differently." Translation thus becomes a stage, where a variety of bodies could assemble temporarily—at times conflictually, often joyfully—to unlearn together and rehearse other ways of being, and acting, in the world.

Ultimately, what truly matters, I think, are the lasting companionships, or relationships—with texts, tongues, artworks, thoughts, and people—that form around, and are sustained by, the labor of translation; as well as the effects that these relationships have on each of us, and the different collectives that we contribute to. Acknowledging our differences, our biases, our privileges, our misunderstandings, our shifting alliances, and our codependencies is not always comfortable or free from conflict and violence. Translating together destabilizes linguistic assumptions, established knowledges, and firm positions, highlighting and unsettling the differentiated roles that are assigned to us depending on gender, sexual orientation, race, nationality, class, and education. It reveals the way these roles are perpetuated through language and speech acts, and how much work is required to unlearn them individually and collectively. This work demands constant attention, attunement to and engagement with others. It is in that sense that I would like to posit translation as a labor of care—not in the individualistic, commodified sense, but as a collective, political act. It is a work of recuperation, as Donna Haraway would put it: of reclaiming the emancipatory, hospitable power of words and ideas, of listening and tending to diverse positions and experiences, and of catching our breath together, and for each other.

Where We Stand, Where We Slip

Correspondence with
Andrea Ancira

October 11–14, 2024

Dear V.,

It's been over one year since we planned a conversation that has not yet taken place. In the meantime, grief has installed itself in multiple bodies and territories. Grief connected to an ongoing genocide in Gaza, neoliberal extractivism across the globe compounded with the rise of the far right. It is in this context, despite and because of all this, that the urgency to animate this conversation arises. Through this exchange of letters, I hope we can accompany each other and continue weaving together from our places, networks, and communities.

I begin with words. In writing, editing, and translating, words take on a distinctive materiality. They can perform a conventional role, such as communicative, but they also play a poetic and creative one. In any case, for both of these functions, their political significance lies in their transformative potential and also in the way they name and co-articulate shared meanings to narrate ourselves against the backdrop of hegemonic discourses.

I'm thinking of a word that comes up in our conversations very often: community. A word that states, whether administered by the right or the left, seem to instrumentalize in implementing their agendas. For example, you have described how, in the last twenty years, the French government has used it to articulate an Islamophobic discourse. In Mexico, for the past seven years, the left-wing government has used this word in their public programs, thus washing communal practices, rooted in indigenous struggles, of their antagonistic critique of the state.[1] How to resist the dispossession of meaning in nationalist discourses? Should we give up on these words or challenge their meaning and the worlds they produce? In *Pedagogías radicales y arte: experiencias comunales* (Radical pedagogies and art: Communal encounters, 2022), a book I edited for Tumbalacasa Ediciones two years ago, we reclaimed the meaning of this word. In response to the state's "communal" turn, we argued that the very existence of communal institutions hinders state capitalism as a totalizing and unique paradigm of social organization. Communal social practices and relations refuse to reproduce principles such as individualism and private property that foreground capitalism and colonial nation-states while also reaffirming autonomy and freedom in terms of self-determination and interdependence. This antagonistic relationship among communal institutions, capitalism, and state institutions, is never pure and entails negotiation, but it prevents communal

---

[1]   A lot of my learning around communal politics is rooted in indigenous struggles and communal pedagogies such as the Zapatista movement (particularly Mujeres y la Sexta), the Asamblea Nacional de Afectados Ambientales, the Universidad de la Tierra in Oaxaca (Unitierra) and the Universidad Autónoma Comunal de Oaxaca (UACO).

politics from being fully captured or confiscated by corporate or state-sponsored programs or policy.

With these situated exercises of wor(l)ding, Tumbalacasa has slowly started to compose a throbbing lexicon of common notions such as: friction, tension, compost, leakage, communal, and soft resistance. In *Militancia alegre* (*Joyful Militancy*),[2] one of the last books that we collectively translated into Spanish, carla bergman and Nick Montgomery work with what they call "common notions," ideas in motion that derive from a collective understanding of what sustains transformation and our participation in its unfolding. These emergent words that throb amid situated communities in resistance become crucial in their sustainability and transformation. Common notions, in this sense, are compasses, urgent meanings, shared orientations (even if circumstantial), notions that can be crooked, reoriented, or reconfigured according to the pulse of our collectivities and intimacies. These common notions do not preexist, they are woven as we go along. They seek to undo certain habits, but avoid moral demands, romanticization, and ideals. In any case, they are flexible principles for action.

For example, the word "tension" means literally to be stretched tight. Although we have been socialized to avoid tension and pathologize it, counterintuitively this

2   carla bergman and Nick Montgomery, *Militancia alegre. Tejer resistencias, florecer en tiempos tóxicos*, trans. Alex K., Alejandra Lagarde, Vero Zoss, Ali González, Jochi, Andrea Ancira, Pablo Martínez, Stefanía Acevedo, Alf Bojórquez, Mercurio Cadena, Pamela Carmona, Olmo Balam (Mexico City: Tumbalacasa Ediciones / Traficantes de Sueños, 2022).

notion holds contradiction in a surprising way. Like an elastic band stretched tight, according to adrianne maree brown, contradiction precipitates such tension within movements that can push our boundaries and the bounds of what we believe is possible.[3] In that stretching, we may widen our capacity to hold oppositional truths, we may contract in response to the exertion, and/or we may build so much pressure within the system that the boundaries that once held us can no longer sustainably contain us and eventually burst. Tension is an image to see us, to feel us, and to understand us in motion, widening, and contracting as individuals and as a collective.

This image of tension and how it holds contradiction was particularly helpful when we published *Lugar de enunciación* (*Where We Stand*) by Djamila Ribeiro,[4] an Afro-Brazilian philosopher and writer whose research and activism has focused on feminist antiracist struggles. We published the Spanish translation of her first book in 2023, almost ten years after it was originally published in Portuguese. In this book, the author develops the concept of a "speaking place" by drawing on the thought of Black feminist theorists who have examined the intertwining of racism and patriarchy. Hand in hand with Grada Kilomba, Sueli Carneiro, Jota Mombaca, Lélia Gonzalez, Patricia Hill Collins, Audre Lorde, Linda Alcoff, Sojourner Truth, Gaytari Spivak, and bell hooks, the author addresses the historical epistemic delegitimization of Black women and

3   adrienne maree brown, *We Will Not Cancel Us; and Other Dreams of Transformative Justice* (Chico, CA: AK Press, 2020), 17.

4   Djamila Ribeiro, *Lugar de enunciación*, trans. Aline Pereira da Encarnação (Mexico City: Tumbalacasa Ediciones, 2023).

challenges the alleged universality of white, bourgeois, Protestant, heterosexual feminism. Despite this book's relevant contribution toward a decolonial genealogy of what is known as standpoint feminism, it was still difficult to get a hold of it in other languages at the time we published it. Fortunately, this work has now been translated into English, German, and French.

The tension in this project emerged as some allegations of transphobia made against the author came to our attention. This happened some months before the book was printed. Our position as a transfeminist publishing platform situated us at a crossroads that quickly turned into an impasse. After questioning whether to cancel the project or not, we decided to dwell in this contradiction and let the tension play itself out. After a series of exchanges with friends and colleagues, we refused to navigate this tension as a moral battle between "good feminist" or "bad feminist" (assuming these are fixed and immutable positions). In a country that denies its Black heritage, where feminist genealogies detached from the liberal feminist narrative are systematically rendered invisible, and where widespread violence and discrimination against trans and gender-diverse people is experienced on a daily basis, we acknowledged the multiple ways in which this book could provoke urgent debates and discussions around racism but also transphobia in feminist movements, despite or even precisely because the author's standpoint was being challenged. Perhaps canceling the project would have ultimately stifled any potential dialogue or debate, while at the same time it would have fed a colonial conception of political congruence informed by a sense of purity and devoid of a space for ambiguity or mistakes that we refuse to embody. In the end, our translations are not driven by a liberal "inclusive" politics but rather a fugitive agency of contamination and self-critical agitation in order to intensely and vitally inhabit a space-time of friction. Liberation struggles are messy and there is no such a thing as pure innocence, therefore we acted in acknowledgment of the discomforts and contradictions on which solidarity is based.

This brings to my mind what Aruna D'Souza calls "imperfect solidarity" as a possible roadmap to reimagine the terms in how and why we come together, clearing a space for transformation.[5] Against the backdrop of a liberal understanding of solidarity based on emotional identification, empathy, understanding, self-righteousness, transparency, and unity, D'Souza calls for forms of political connection based on temporary, context-specific alliances that allow difference and even contradiction to remain intact while understanding such contradiction as a strength, not a weakness. As I reflect on these experiences, I realize that every project with its corresponding tensions has compelled us to embrace complexity as part of the work of putting ourselves in relation to others. It is a dance between difference and communality, an improvised choreography in which listening, as a feminist tool, becomes fundamental—isn't it?

5   Aruna D'Souza, *Imperfect Solidarities* (Berlin: Floating Opera Press, 2024).

Can't wait to hear more about how and with whom you dance this dance in the creative, familial, and pedagogical contexts that shape your current life.

Sending you love from my little cave in Vienna's 17th district,

Andrea

November 21–22, 2024

Queridx Andrea,

More than one month has passed since you wrote me this letter. Part of me feels guilty for letting it go unattended for so long, although I have been sensing its presence, your presence—a companionship, a comradeship, a carefulness that exists like a river, continuously running, even underground, even without words or signs. You are there, I am thinking and dancing with you, trusting the generative force that our friendship carries on across distances and absences. Another part of me refused to open the letter before a moment would come when I could dedicate the time and attention I knew it deserved to reading and answering it. I did not want this correspondence to turn into a pending item on my to-do list, into yet another work-related pressure—although we have regularly used professional invitations as occasions to meet and think together, from the first exchange of letters published in the collective publication *Co-Creation* in 2019,[6] to the beautiful exercises on "translucination" that you offered

6   Céline Poulin and Marie Preston, with Stéphanie Airaud, eds., *Co-Creation* (Paris: Éditions Empire, 2019).

as part of the "Gestures of Untranslatability" program in 2023.[7] Today that moment has come, a mix of planning and coincidence: an unexpected snowstorm has hit the northwestern part of France, where I live—where it rarely snows, especially in November. I am watching the snowflakes whirling in silence, covering the trees, swings, cabbages, henhouse: perfect weather for writing to a friend. It carries a sense of wonder and softness, of isolation and concentration, as well as a feeling of apprehensiveness—I almost slid off the road this morning, and I am worried about driving back from school with Nour and Farah later this afternoon on the unsalted forest road.

This year, I decided to join the group of elected parent representatives who act as intermediaries between families, the school (a small countryside school welcoming around ninety children between three and ten years old), and the city council. I did so after the far right won 40 percent of the local vote in the European elections last May. During the ensuing campaign for legislative elections in France, after President Macron dissolved the

---

[7] "Gestures of Untranslatability" was a weeklong module of workshops, presentations, and collective activities, conceived by Virginie Bobin and Vir Andres Hera (Qalqalah قلقلة) on the invitation of UNIDEE Visiting Curator Chiara Cartuccia as part of her two-year project "Neither on Land Nor at Sea. Meeting by the Mediterranean Im/Possible," hosted by UNIDEE Residency Programs and Cittadellarte – Fondazione Pistoletto in Biella, Italy. It took place from 11–17 December, 2024. The collective publication *Sorry, I Didn't Understand. Can You Say That Again? Notes on Gestures of Untranslatability*, including the collective "translucination" produced during Andrea Ancira's workshop, is available at https://qalqalah.org /en/notes-on/sorry-i-didnt-understand.

National Assembly, I strongly felt the lack of a space of encounter and debate in the village: no café, no central square, no shop, only our closest neighbors, who luckily align with our political views and shared our anger and fear, while racist and homophobic acts were raising across the country. Where could we, a serendipitous community of villagers with divergent political opinions and worldviews, collectively challenge the words that we were using or receiving, analyze public discourses, and test our supposed differences and commonalities? And where we, my partner and I, could question our own position as highly educated, financially stable, cultural workers who made the choice to relocate to a beautiful rural area with a certain degree of privileges and ideals? The group of parent representatives belatedly presented itself as a space of encounter, negotiation, and confrontation, where discussions about such topics as security, authority, discipline, harassment, health, care, celebration, and togetherness are held among persons with very different perspectives and, at times, divergent vocabularies. A space, albeit modest, where the fabric of community itself is at play, full of misunderstandings, disagreement, surprises, and imagination. A space of tension.

I wanted to thank you for sharing your reflections and revisiting some of the experiences of tension that recently marked your publishing, editing, and translating work with such generosity and thoughtfulness. As always, your words are precise, uncompromising, and open at the same time. You remind the reader that failure, mistakes, doubts, and vulnerability are not turnoffs; they demand that we continue the work. They also demand that we take responsibility for that work, and that is where the collective—a configuration that both of us hold dear in many aspects of our lives—offers such a precious, necessary framework of contradiction, plurality, and support. I have written at length about how Qalqalah قلقلة represents both a space of confrontation and refuge, where we can find the collective strength to act beyond and with our dissensus—as we did when we organized a series of fundraiser screenings for Palestine last year, or collectively translated a speech by Palestinian writer Mohammed El-Kurd on Gaza on March 8, the global feminist strike day.[8] It was a drop in the ocean, of course, and nothing to brag about. What I want to stress is the potential in collective configurations for overcoming our feelings of sideration and helplessness through the collectivization of despair and rage.

In response to your letter, and in continuation of the thread I began to pull with the school as a space of tension, I want to revisit a recent experience that took place in a pedagogical context. The (art) school is yet another space that we have practiced together, since you are also conducting research as part of the PhD in Practice at the Academy of Fine Arts in Vienna, where my own reflections on translation and untranslatability took shapes.

In January 2024, Anne Kerzerho, a long-term interlocutor and the pedagogical director of the Exerce master's degree in choreography at ICI-CCN in

---

8   "Mohammed El-Kurd à propos de Gaza," Qalqalah قلقلة, March 8, 2024, https://qalqalah.org/fr/notes-sur/mohammed-el-kurd-a-propos-de-gaza.

Montpellier, invited Myriam Suchet and I to conduct a workshop for first-year students that addressed translation, learning, working, and commoning across a variety of languages. Indeed, the seven students (most of whom have a professional background in performance and choreography) came from a variety of international contexts, some strongly marked by colonial histories and continuums. When joining the program, students commit to work in French and English, two (imperial) languages that are "unequally shared among the group, who speak, write and dance many other languages" (in Myriam's words). This situation repeats every year, as the exerce is one of the rare French pedagogical programs to embrace an international scope in the selection of participants and guests as well as the curriculum. Anne's invitation testified to a desire to address this from an institutional, systemic perspective, and perhaps forge tools that could be useful for the program in the long run. During one preparatory meeting, I joked that Myriam and I would act as a crisis unit for language-related issues. It turned out to be the case, and it was not a joke.

In the book, I argue that practicing translation and untranslatability can offer tools for collective care and resistance, particularly in pedagogical contexts. For the master's students, the daily responsibility of translation often fell on their shoulders, who had to improvise makeshift translations depending on the language spoken by a guest, for example. This was experienced as a weight for both the translators and the translated, something that enhanced inequalities in the distribution of speech and knowledge; something that took energy and time away from what they came to do in the program. When Myriam and I joyfully introduced our work with languages and offered translation games as a starting point for the workshop, we were immediately confronted with a lot of pain, exasperation, and exhaustion. "Translation is not a game for me," a student said. "It is a disability."

We had three days to work together, plus another two days later in May (we had asked ICI-CCN to invite us a second time, to provide continuity). First of all, Myriam and I offered to take charge of French/English translations throughout the entire workshop. We either interpreted what each other had said orally, or one of us typed the contents of our discussions live in the other language using a shared online text editor, which appeared on a screen behind us (we did not include names, as some personal things were shared). Although the students sometimes jumped in to translate as well, they later told us what a relief it was to have translation taken care of by the guests, and that it was put on the table from the start, instead of just being the elephant in the room. Each time a new session began, we collectively decided how it would be translated, and by whom. This led us to work on a repertory of gestures (notably inspired by those used to collectively moderating discussions in activist contexts) that could be activated by the group, and shared with the exerce faculty and external guests to raise awareness and call for more attentiveness around the distribution of language in the program. One gesture particularly struck me. It signifies: "I don't need translation." It was requested by the only person who did not speak English and was thus often perceived by the rest of the group to be excluded from the conversations. The only Black person in the room, too. Often, the group would turn to him when translation occurred or ask him if he needed translation. He said that he did not want the rest of the group to feel constantly responsible for him and that, at times, he wanted to be able to refuse translation, to experience the situation without translation, or simply to retreat.

Our conversations revolved a lot about the power relations at play in the translation process, both interpersonal and institutional. The students' interventions were sharp, subtle, and caring: "Could translation just remain a problem, instead of being turned into an occasion for creation?" "Translation is not a tool, it is a relation. It is emotionally engaging." "When I translate here, I do not provide a service. I am not being paid for it. We need to be co-responsible for translation." "The institution needs to be responsible too." "How to make it lighter for each other?" "How close is it to a matter of life and death?" And my personal favorite: "How do we apply tender tools in untender situations?"

Myriam and I mostly listened: gave a few prompts, received, translated, transcribed, but mostly listened. I have never felt so close to being in a therapeutic role—so conscious of the responsibility that this kind of position entails, of the exhaustion it provokes, of my shortcomings and, actually, of what I was able to offer through the experience I gained in these years of untranslating with others (learning to be a feminist ear, you know?). Translation was both the problem and the resource, it was inescapable in both instances, even when it was refused or voluntarily corrupted. The whole thing worked out because translation became a kind of common notion, as you described, a place and a compass around which a temporary collective could be formed and performed. With a compelling tenderness.

I wrote them a letter, you know. It is composed of fragments from our conversations, in Frenchenglishes. It was thought as a gift to them, to thank them for all that we had (un)learned together in translation. We read and edited it collectively during the second workshop in May, during which we spoke about their own work, drifting away from the weight of translation, and shared a lot of food. The letter was published, alongside the repertory of gestures and a "translation kit," in the last volume of *Traduire du français aux français*, a collection of booklets edited by Myriam Suchet.[9] We wanted to leave a trace of our encounter and a set of possible tools that may be used by others, future exerce students, teachers, activists—whoever is confronted with translation in a collective context.

As you know, two months ago I officially became a teacher: I joined the local school of fine arts as a professor in art and social practice, with an approach based on theory and practice. The art school context, with all its complexities and ambiguities, is where I want to continue this work, although I am struggling a lot with the power that I now hold—and, again, the responsibility

9   Virginie Bobin, "Walking Through the Trouble in Translation," in Myriam Suchet, *Traduire du français aux français*, no. 9 (Rennes: éditions du commun, 2024). The letter is also available at https://qalqalah.org/en /conversations/cheminer-le-trouble-en-traduction.

that comes with it. My courses are not about languages and translation, but what I have learned as a translatress definitely irrigates the dialogical, collective, and caring pedagogical praxis that I am trying to elaborate in conversation with the students, where attention to words is central. Last week, two students, Xinyi Shen and Mengting Wang, came to see me: they wanted advice to start a pirate Chinese languages course inside the school, both as an artistic project and to point out the structural inequalities and exclusions they have faced since arriving in France for their studies. They are humorous and determined. I can't wait to witness what tender tools they will forge to survive untender situations.

With much love my dear friend, thank you for writing and inviting me to dance with your words once more,

V.

February 2025

Dear V.,

This time it took me longer to answer. I received your letter on the shores of Lake Atitlán—it is said to be the deepest lake in Central America—surrounded by three volcanoes: San Pedro, Tolimán, and Atitlán. These volcanic peaks watch over the lake, encircled by a belt of hills that plunge steeply into the turquoise, emerald, or glassy waters, depending on the light that touches its 130-square-kilometer surface. It is one of those few spots where I feel at home. Also, it was in these hills, over thirty years ago, that my stepfather lived in a guerrilla camp during Guatemala's counterinsurgency war.

I was attending the seminar "Trabajo, creación y memoria o cómo se reproduce la vida comunalmente" (Labor, creation, and memory, or how life is reproduced communally), organized by Proyecto Parutz' and curated by Gladys Tzul Tzul. As with your courses, this seminar was not about translation, but translation happened in most of the sessions, since most of the group didn't know the Mayan languages spoken by the presenters. A few days before the winter solstice, we gathered to learn how communal politics and the affective texture of a grieving caring commons are intertwined with cycles of life and harvests in Iximulew.[10] As you know, for the past year, I have been enduring a personal loss, but also, my PhD research delves into the social, political, and aesthetic relations that collective loss creates and adheres to in the present, specifically in postwar Guatemala. In this setting, it became clear to what extent creation serves the political work of mourning.

This brings me to the interventions from the exerce students, two in particular that have stayed with me: the one thoughtfully questioning whether translation should be seen merely as a problem, rather than an opportunity for creation; and another reflecting on translation as a form of disability. After almost four years of living and working in Vienna without speaking German (or Viennese), I could somehow relate to both. For those who depend on translation on a daily basis, most of our life experiences are teeming with it: friendships, work, love, activism, sex, bureaucracy, and a long etcetera. Being dependent on (mis)translation everyday can create a sense of failure and shame. If, alongside this, we are asked to address that condition in a creative or productive way in an institutional setting that often overlooks the systemic violence at its core, while also reproducing and intensifying them through individualization, it is inevitable that the contradiction gets fully exposed—in this case,

---

10   *Iximulew* is an expression from the K'iche' Maya language meaning "land of corn," and their ancestral name for what is today known as Guatemala.

either through exhaustion or frustration. In a so-called postcolonial world marked by migration, forced displacement, and land dispossession, why do states and schools continue to insist that translation is not an intrinsic, universal part of existence, but instead a shameful reflection of our personal failure?

With the acknowledgment of my own stake in this topic, I read with great interest and a sense of curiosity about the workshops you and Myriam conducted. From what I gather, it seems that—similar to the seminar in Guatemala, where creation was at the service of collective mourning—in this case, creation was at the service of the political work of translation, and not the other way around. Instead of simply managing a problem to be fixed (as is often the case in institutional settings), the care and attentiveness both of you brought to that space, along with the students' willingness to actively engage with the prompts, allowed you to craft generous opportunities for "staying with the trouble." I have always deeply admired the way you navigate and work within the cracks of institutions, whether in academic settings like this recent case or in exhibition spaces (as I witnessed at Villa Vassilieff). It is precisely from these cracks that institutions reveal their potential to be more porous, allowing space for a hospitality that defies conventional norms and opens up possibilities for more inclusive, transformative practices.

Now that you have a more permanent role as a professor at an art school, I look forward to hearing more about the many tender tools and common languages like Frenchenglishes (not tied to land or country but to movement, migration, and spaces in-between) that emerge, both in and outside the classroom, to survive but also to transform untender situations and contexts.

In solidarity, and esperando que nos sigamos acompañando en estas tenues resistencias.

Yours truly,

Andrea

Authors: Andrea Ancira, Virginie Bobin
Editors: Alice Dusapin and Sophie Orlando (scientific editor)
Collection: Scratching the Surface
Design: In the shade of a tree   Copyediting: Zoe Harris
ISBN: 978-1-915609-83-0   Printing: INNI   Typefaces: Feld (MA-MA Type), Signifier (Klim Type)
All rights reserved, including the right of reproduction in whole or in part in any form
Distributed by The MIT Press, Art Data, Les presses du réel, and Idea Books
EU Authorised Representative: Easy Access System Europe, Mustamäe tee 50, 10621 Tallinn, Estonia
gpsr.request@easproject.com
Published by Sternberg Press, 71–75 Shelton Street, London WC2H 9JQ, www.sternberg-press.com
and Villa Arson, 20 Av. Stephen Liegard, 06100 Nice

Editorial Assistant: Norma Conroux

© 2025 Virginie Bobin, Villa Arson

scratching

the

surface

SternbergPress

villa
arson

nice

lasurfacedemange

villa-arson